A House Divided:

Evangelicals and the Establishment in Hull 1770 – 1914

Peter Stubley

THE UNIVERSITY OF HULL PRESS

Monograph in Regional and Local History

A House Divided:
Evangelicals and the Establishment in Hull
1770 – 1914

THE UNIVERSITY OF HULL PRESS

© Peter Stubley

British Library Cataloguing in Publication Data

A catalogue record for this book is available from the British Library

ISBN 0 85958 633 2
ISSN 0951 8916

Published 1995

Phototypeset in 11 on 12pt Palatino by Gem DTP, 37 Hunter Road, Elloughton, HU15 1LG and printed by the Central Print Unit, the University of Hull.

Contents

Acknowledgements

I am indebted to many conversations with people in Hull in preparing this study, including teachers, local historians, and authors of works on Hull. In particular my thanks are due to the staff of the Local Studies Department at Hull Central Library, to Humberside County Record Office, Hull City Record Office and Hull City Museums. The City and County are rich in archives and research materials and their staffs are always pleased to point them out to the student. In addition, the shelves of the Brynmor Jones Library at The University of Hull contain some rare treasures donated and preserved over many years for today's researcher. This book began as a Ph.D thesis for the University of Durham, presented in 1991, and supervised by Dr Sheridan Gilley, whom I also wish to thank most warmly.

Abbreviations

HCL	Hull Central Library
HCR (HRO)	Hull City Records
HMGB	*A History of the Methodist Church in Great Britain*
LEMP	*Lives of the Early Methodist Preachers*
VCH	*The Victoria History of the County of York East Riding*, Volume I
WMM	*Wesleyan Methodist Magazine*

Foreword

Introduction

In an age when Churches appeal for reconciliation among peoples divided by race or ethnicity, it is salutary to remember that in nineteenth-century Europe religion was a major source of conflict. This was true of many Western European societies, but nowhere more so than in Hull. This book charts the virulent and tragic history of that conflict.

Until about 1770, English cities still presented a contrast to the countryside, where handicraft, cottage industries and the alliance of squire and parson still maintained a social system where the Anglican settlement of 1660 was maintained. Urban life was more pluralist, and Anglican hegemony was much less great in cities such as Hull, throughout the century. However, in the late eighteenth century Hull began to expand rapidly as a port for the industrial cities of Yorkshire. At the same time an evangelical revival stirred the religious life of the city. The combination of rapid commercial expansion, a large class of those in constant poverty and insecurity, and religious rivalry, led to an uneasy society in Victorian Hull. Robert Southey wrote of the growth of industrial England that 'a manufacturing populace is always rife for rioting . . . Governments who found their prosperity upon manufactures sleep upon gunpowder'. This was certainly the fear of Hull merchants after 1815. Ever reminiscent of the French Revolution, they sought to tame the poor, while preserving a religious struggle that was a constant source of social tension and prevented real co-operation in tackling serious urban problems.

In this fascinating study, Peter Stubley traces the social and religious conflict of the city of Hull in the century and a half before World War One. He analyses the strategies for social reform, such as education, temperance, the suppression of prostitution and Sunday trading. Hull was a great Evangelical city, yet the poverty which accompanied economic growth defied social reform. At the same time competition between the churches for membership only entrenched further divisions between the middle classes. The anti-Catholicism of early Victorian Hull eventually died away, as did the fear of revolution, but the bitter struggle over education remained until 1914.

It is an absorbing, if sobering, story of 'a house divided'. Peter Stubley is well equipped to tell the narrative. He has taught in the University of Hull, worked as an industrial chaplain in the city, and collaborated with industrialists, churches, politicians and trade unionists in many projects of social regeneration. Today Hull is in rapid change from an industrial port to a more diverse existence as a retail, service and industrial centre. The predominant climate is secular, with a social consensus which supports local government intervention to reshape Hull for the next century.

This study tells a very different story of intense religious feeling, bitter social division and equally rapid social and economic change. In all of this the churches sought to improve the everyday life of the people of Hull, although their controversies often provided room for suspicion. The ambiguity of religious life is vividly portrayed through its leading protagonists. Nineteenth-century Hull was anything but dull; and this study brings it to life in a graphic way. It is at one and the same time a tragic and inspiring, but always compelling, story.

Peter Sedgwick,
Westcott House,
Cambridge

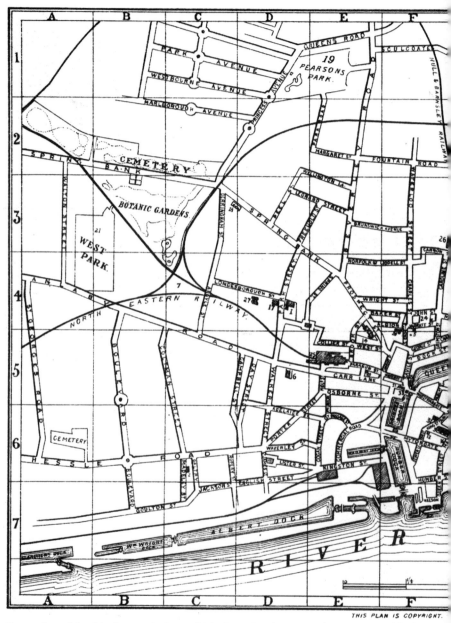

Reproduced by kind permission of Mr Pye (Books), Local History Publishers

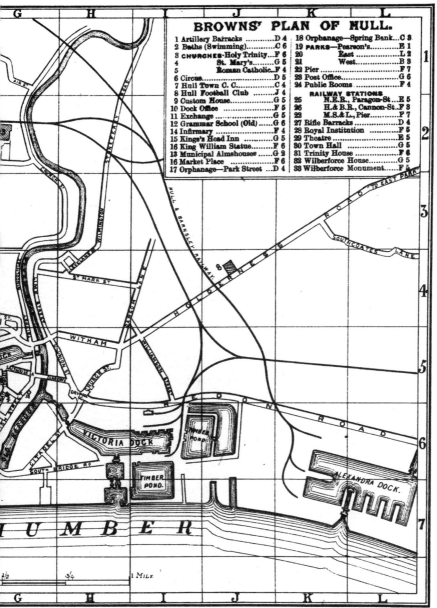

I

An Evangelical City

Hull has the reputation of being an irreligious town. The propagation of religion over the last two hundred years provoked a comparatively indifferent response and produced meagre results for all the main-stream Christian denominations. Recent statistics placed the county of Humberside at the bottom of the national league table for church attendance.[1]

The Evangelical revival was a world-wide phenomenon, affecting religious life from Eastern Europe to the north-east coast of the United States of America in the eighteenth and nineteenth centuries.[2] This study will explore some of the ways in which Evangelicalism in the Church of England attempted to work out its ideals in Hull during the same period. Hull's Evangelicals aimed to convert a rapidly developing commercial town and port into a model Evangelical city. In one respect the religious inclinations of the town looked promising; since the English Civil War and its aftermath, Hull had been predominantly Protestant and Puritan, fertile ground, it might have been thought, for a religious outlook which lay special stress on personal conversion, salvation by faith, the verbal inspiration and sole authority of Scripture, and the supreme importance of preaching.

There were, however, three strands or types of Evangelicalism, Church of England, Dissenting, and Methodist, and although they had much in common, their effectiveness was greatly weakened by denominational rivalry and differences involving politics and class. Arguably the greatest stumbling block preventing co-operation among Christians of similar religious outlook was the establishment of the Church of England and all that establishment entailed, socially and politically.

Evangelicals may not have been a majority in the Church of England in the eighteenth century, but they were a notable group within it. Among other denominations affected by the eighteenth-century Evangelical revival were the Independents, later called Congregationalists, and the Methodists, followers of John Wesley who later broke away from the Church of England after Wesley's death in 1791. Independents and Methodists were the strongest representatives of Nonconformity in nineteenth-century Hull. At first Independency was the stronger, but before the end of the century Methodism, subdivided into various strands of its own, was by far the stronger and the town's largest single religious group.

Evangelicals in the Church of England believed that its establishment was vital for the safety and well-being of the whole nation. The political and religious bedrock for them was the settlement of 1689 which followed the 'Glorious Revolution' in 1688 when William of Orange became King William III of England. From henceforth the monarch's coronation oath guaranteed the 'Protestant religion' as the religion of the English people and of the Church of England.

'Protestant' might be a classification acceptable to all who were not Roman Catholics, but had been defined more exclusively before 1689, to the Church of England's advantage, by the Corporation Act of 1661 and the Test Act of 1673. The former required all members of municipal corporations to take an oath of allegiance and to affirm that they had received the sacrament of Holy Communion according to the rites of the Church of England within the preceding year. The Test Act also required all office holders under the crown to receive the sacrament according to the usage of the Church of England. Dissenting ministers and schoolmasters were required to subscribe to the Thirty-nine Articles until 1779, but the Test and Corporation Acts were not repealed until 1828; the following year Catholic Emancipation was passed, at last permitting Roman Catholics to sit in Parliament.

Evangelicals in Hull at the turn of the century were not alone in suspecting the political motives of Dissenters and Roman Catholics, but the longevity of the Evangelical clergy helped to ensure that their suspicions were also long-lived. Dissenters had sympathised with the cause of the French Revolution in its earliest stages, and ever after they were suspected of political radicalism. There is evidence that political distrust of Nonconformity lasted in Hull at least until the First World War.

Roman Catholics were seen as representatives of a foreign power, intent on overthrowing both Church and State. The Church of England would be replaced by the Church of Rome, it was feared, and a Catholic monarch would sit on England's Protestant throne if Catholics had their way. Catholic Emancipation in 1829 and the restoration of a Catholic hierarchy in England in 1850 were causes of great alarm for Church of England Evangelicals.

This threat from both sides, as it appeared to the Church of England, precluded the possibility of an alliance with Nonconformity to resist Catholicism and provide for the religious and social needs of the growing town. Nonconformists in Hull were no sympathisers with Catholic doctrine and church order, but ironically they were fellows in adversity with Catholics, outside the status and privileges which belonged exclusively to the Established Church.

Hull's Church of England clergy spent much of their time and energy in the first half of the nineteenth century resisting what they saw as the unwarranted political and religious claims of Catholicism, but for the whole of the century they defended the old order against the alleged political and social threats of Nonconformity. The fear of political radicalism survived until the eclipse of the Liberal Party in the 1920s, but what turned out to be the final battle was fought over the elementary education of the poor. Nonconformity and the Established Church had learned to live with each other after the Education Act of 1870 in a kind of armed truce, but hostilities broke out with greater virulence on the passing of the Conservative Education Act in 1902. The war was finally lost for Nonconformity when the Liberal Education Bill was withdrawn from the House of Commons in 1906. The Church of England, now more influential than ever, looked forward to enjoying the fruits of its victory.

II

The Beginning of a Dynasty

There were one or two other Evangelical clergy in the Church of England in Hull in the eighteenth century, but the life and work of the Revd Joseph Milner, headmaster of Hull Grammar School from 1767 to 1797, marked the start of an unbroken Evangelical dynasty. He and his immediate successors ensured that Evangelicalism became and was to remain the dominant feature of the Established Church in Hull.

Two concerns were symptomatic of Milner's ministry. His initial warmth towards Dissenters, so similar to himself in religious outlook, soon cooled when they showed sympathy towards radical politics, especially during the early stages of the French Revolution. In this he was at one not only with other Evangelicals but with all who counted themselves as 'Church of England.' Secondly, Milner's thirty years in Hull witnessed the early stages of its transformation from a medieval town into a rapidly growing modern port and commercial city. He deplored the exuberant commercialism which militated against the religious values he preached and multiplied the labouring classes who were increasingly indifferent to organized religion.

Joseph Milner and his younger brother Isaac were the sons of a poor weaver in Leeds. They were both exceptionally intelligent and attended Leeds Grammar School until their father's death in 1762. As a result Isaac Milner, still only twelve years of age, was obliged to become a weaver's apprentice but Joseph, six years older, entered St Catherine's College Cambridge through the support of a group of Leeds business men who were anxious to ensure an education for such a promising young man.

After Cambridge, Milner became assistant master at the Revd Christopher Atkinson's school at Thorpe Arch, taking holy orders in 1766 to become Atkinson's curate. The following year he applied for the post of headmaster at Hull Grammar School and at the interview won the approval of two Aldermen, the Mayor Francis Pryme and William Wilberforce, grandfather of the famous Emancipator.[1] With an income to support himself he took his brother away from the loom, brought him to Hull and prepared him for University. Neither of the brothers married, and when Isaac later became President of Queens' College Cambridge and Dean of Carlisle he still regarded the school house at Hull as his home until the end of Joseph's life.

At first Joseph, not yet an Evangelical, lived up to his employers' expectations. He was rewarded with the chaplaincy of Lister's Hospital, an almshouse dating from 1642; the school house was repaired and his stipend increased from £30 to £40 a year. In addition to these duties he was also afternoon lecturer at Holy Trinity Church and curate of North Ferriby.

Milner experienced an Evangelical conversion in 1770. His adoption of 'methodistical' views, as they were called at that time, was said by some to be the result of attending a meeting of Lady Huntingdon's student-evangelists in Fish Street Independent Church. Lady Huntingdon founded a body of Calvinistic Methodists known as the Countess of Huntingdon's Connexion. She had joined the Wesleys' Methodist Society in

1739 and was the chief means of introducing Methodism to the upper classes. Milner himself attributed his conversion to reading the Anglican divine Richard Hooker's (died 1600) *On Justification*.[2]

Whatever the cause, Milner's new outlook lost him the support of Hull's leading citizens. They did not like his 'serious' views on religion and stayed away when he preached in Holy Trinity, except for his annual sermon as Mayor's Chaplain. They no longer invited him to their houses and some removed their children from his school, among them Alderman Wilberforce who threatened that 'if Billy turns Methodist he shall not have a sixpence of mine'.[3] It was noticed that 'few persons who wore a tolerably good coat would take notice of him when they met him in the street'.[4] He gave up playing cards and no longer went to the theatre or assembly rooms where he had once looked for an opportunity to 'say a word in season.' His admonitions made men ill at ease and 'the man who had become insupportable in the pulpit ceased to become a desirable guest at the table'.[5]

Over the years Milner slowly came back into favour. The people of Ferriby noticed how he came to see them in fair weather and in foul. His pupils at the Grammar School became leaders of Hull society and Evangelical ideas were becoming more acceptable generally. Eventually, 'no clergyman was well received in Hull who opposed or did not support them'.[6]

Milner seems to have had more success with the daughters of Hull's merchants, since Evangelical clergymen came from far and wide to court them as wives with suitable theological opinions. Sometimes there was jealousy and rivalry and one clergyman was incensed when a rival spoke first for the young woman he had in mind for himself. Local marriage registers record that the Revd John Venn married William King's daughter Kitty in 1789. Henry Thornton, the Evangelical banker and member of the 'Clapham Sect', married Marianne Sykes in 1796 and the Revd Edward Edwards, a friend of John Venn, married Anne Pead in 1796.

The chief vehicle of Milner's public ministry in Hull was his preaching and about 800 of his sermons were published. He was described as 'a Boanerges of the pulpit . . . with (his) massy form, grave countenance, a weighty manner, and a strong unmusical voice'.[7] His Grammar School pupils who saw another side of his character retained affectionate memories of him, but to those who only knew him from his manner in the pulpit he appeared severe and morose.

It was Milner's uncompromising otherworldliness which most upset Hull's men of business. He saw great moral dangers in Britain's increasing economic wealth; it was the main cause of a growing neglect of God on the part of those engaged in a life of commercial gain. During Milner's thirty years in Hull the population doubled, but his inflexible convictions allowed no quarter and he saw in the new world growing up around him a deadly threat to 'serious religion'.

The new wealth made possible a glittering social life for the town's elite; William Wilberforce described Hull in the 1770s as one of the gayest places outside London.[8] Milner's response was a never-ending onslaught on the new degeneracy from the pulpit of Holy Trinity, and the conviction of sin, the primary teaching of Scripture as he saw it, provided him with enough ammunition to bombard believers, unbelievers and nominal Christians alike. In Hull, Milner detected 'a proud and worldly spirit and the excessive love of gain eating out the love of Christ'. He saw 'the awful progress of gross wickedness and vice, of lewdness and impiety', which in his judgement were the results of the 'rapid increase in commerce, in wealth, in population, in building and in luxury',[9] all the obvious outward aspects of any growing seaport.

Milner urged Christians to give as little time as possible to public life, except 'to pray for the peace of Jerusalem and seek its good . . . to be subject to the principalities and powers, to obey the magistrates, and to be ready for every good work'.[10] Evangelicals in the Established Church were usually Tory in politics so Milner performed his duty as he saw it 'as a subject of the King', but did not offer a religious apologetic for worldly success. Hull's merchants might have put up with his public denunciation of their sins if he had at least allowed them that much.[11]

Milner did not undervalue this world completely but saw it as a training ground for the next. His experience as an eighteenth-century bachelor schoolmaster encouraged him to regard it as a harsh training ground. Strict instruction and firm discipline were equally necessary at school and at home, he said, and parents should not be afraid of hurting their offspring by labour of body and mind. 'Youth must be inured to labour from an early age in order to be free from the evils of sloth in manhood'.[12] He was thinking of the children of the well-to-do who were likely to have at least some association with church and clergy. The children of the 'dregs of the poor', as he called them, were less easy to reach or influence. They had been 'abandoned by unprincipled parents and naturally learned and followed every evil'; there was little hope for them humanly speaking, 'except by the friendly aid of charity schools or of similar institutions'.[13]

Every section of the community - men of wealth, merchants, sailors and labourers - was castigated by Milner for its irreligious worldliness and its indifference to the coming judgement.[14] The coarse language of the poor made them doubly offensive to him.[15] Milner's constant refrain was of the transcience of this life, the certainty of judgement and the reality of hell. The parable of Dives and Lazarus[16] convinced him that if happiness was thought to be found in this world's goods, we should experience 'unspeakable disappointment and confusion' in the world to come.[17] But lest the poor thought this let them off lightly, Milner told them that they would not be happy hereafter 'merely because they were miserable in this life'.[18]

It was unlikely that many of Hull's merchants could ever hope to qualify as Milner's model man of God, especially if they were expected to concern themselves with only what was essential or unavoidable in this world. Yet Milner believed that this world had its purpose. He spoke of the 'temporal advantages of godliness' which enabled one 'to bear temporal evils with cheerfulness and joy'.[19] Labour and temperance united, he said, resulted in good health, enabling the godly man to redeem the time, do the work God had set him to do and 'be useful to his fellow creatures'.[20]

There is truth in this point of view, but many were to discover that a combination of labour and temperance had a habit of accumulating the very riches which Milner deplored. Thus the process which beguiled so many from the narrow path of righteousness was repeated in the next generation.

Evangelicals were not unaware of this dilemma; the Puritan ethic of success in business as a sign of God's approval was of little avail in a society increasingly absorbed by Evangelical values. Christ's warning against the perils of riches and his precepts on the superiority of poverty set the huge money-making enterprises of the age against its intense religious feelings. The rich saw it was their duty to keep the poor in order, but they could be equally severe on themselves over the accumulation of wealth. The poor might be dissolute and feckless, but the rich regarded themselves as in greater spiritual danger through their increasing investments.[21]

The vicar of Holy Trinity, the Revd Arthur Clarke, William Wilberforce's brother-in-law, died in July 1797. Wilberforce came to stay with his sister and took the opportunity to canvass among the aldermen for Joseph Milner's appointment to the vacant living. In his diary for 22 August he wrote, 'Milner appointed vicar by the Corporation. My being there probably got him elected'.[22] On his way to York for his institution, Milner caught a chill and died on 15 November, aged 52. Wilberforce appears to have played no further part in the matter and the Revd John Healey Bromby was instituted as vicar of Holy Trinity. Bromby, who was to remain vicar for seventy years, had been a pupil of Milner at the Grammar School; he was a Cambridge man but not an Evangelical. Thus the leadership of Hull's Evangelical dynasty passed to the Revd Thomas Dikes, vicar of St John's Church.

Thomas Dikes subscribed to many of Milner's religious and political opinions, but was quite different in character. Of slight build, more graceful, less stern, a preacher in much gentler mould, less doctrinal, he addressed himself to the kindly feelings of human nature.[23] He was a decided Evangelical, but a moderate Calvinist who believed that divine grace and human responsibility were reconcilable. Nevertheless he was equally opposed to radical politics and to Dissent.

Dikes, born in Ipswich in 1761, turned to religion after a serious illness in his youth and as a result he came to Hull to seek Milner's advice about ordination. He was prepared for University by Edward Garwood, curate at St Mary's, Lowgate, and entered Magdalene College, Cambridge in 1786. Here he came under the influence of Isaac Milner, Charles Simeon, the leading Evangelical in Cambridge, and two undergraduates, John Venn and Robert Jarratt. The latter, from Hull, became a life-long friend and served a curacy near Hull before leaving for a parish in Somerset. Dikes was appointed curate at Cottingham and, so his father hoped, might then have returned to his native Suffolk, but the death of his maiden aunt, Rosa, helped to decide his future. He was attracted by the idea of staying near Milner, so with his aunt's legacy he built St John's Church, the first outside the town walls, on the site of the present Ferens Art Gallery, aiming to recover his outlay from pew rents.

Dikes was a firm believer in the Establishment; to him the Church of England was the bulwark of the nation.[24] Though, like Milner, he was generally on friendly terms with Dissenters in matters of religion, he preferred not to co-operate with anyone who objected to the Establishment of the Church, not even in the distribution of Bibles among the poor. His trust in this 'great moral bulwark' made him conservative in politics with a mistrust of Chartism, Puseyism and Romanism as attempts to subvert the constitution of the nation. Milner feared divine intervention and the collapse of the social order as a result of the wickedness of the people. Dikes expected the same on account of their political and religious perfidy, particularly over concessions to the Roman Catholic claims.

Dikes differed from Milner, however, in his attitude to the modern world of commercial expansion and increasing population. He was on more friendly terms with Hull's leaders and found their world more to his taste, in spite of its even faster growth than in Milner's time. Hull's first modern dock was built in Milner's lifetime; Dikes witnessed the building of three more, one threatening his newly-built church with demolition. The population increased four-fold and Hull was linked to Selby by the rail road. Dikes found all this exhilarating, expressing his joy at the erection of a church 'where a population has increased, is increasing, and may increase to an infinite extent'.[25] When St James' Church was opened in Pottery, a poor district near St John's, Dikes's eulogy endorsed commerce as the glory of the nation. 'Nature gave scope', he said, 'to industry and exertion and called into existence that middle class of society in which was found more of the comfort which blessed, and more of the virtue which embellished civil society'.[26] In just over twenty years Dikes was responsible for, or closely associated with, the building of six churches, three of them opened in successive years, driven on by an urge to provide church accommodation for the town's growing population.

It soon became clear to Dikes and his curates that evangelism was not so successful as they hoped from a population growing chiefly through inward migration. John Scott, Dikes' first curate, wrote to his father Thomas Scott, the Bible commentator, 'We have several Meetings, but they only seem to catch people on whom religion has got some former hold'.[27] Soon after St John's was opened there were about a thousand in the congregation, but it was inevitable that most were of the 'higher class' who could afford an average pew rent of seventeen pounds. Some locked their pew to ensure it remained empty when they were away in the country.[28]

It was one thing to be well-disposed towards businessmen and merchants, and Dissenters up to a point, but Roman Catholics were quite another matter. Dikes feared the surrender of the 'Protestant principle' on which the constitution was based following the accession of William III in 1689. Emancipation, in Dikes' opinion, would not satisfy Catholic aspirations. 'Those who know anything of Popery,' he wrote to a friend in 1828, 'must know that they would never be content till they had a Catholic King, Catholic Bishops, and a Catholic Government'.[29] At the open air meeting in 1829, the year of Catholic Emancipation, Dikes continued to extol the value of throne and government for the good of his country. Puseyism was even worse than Catholicism; it was the enemy within which would admit Catholicism through the back door. 'The more I read the Oxford Tracts,' he wrote in 1833, 'the less I like them.' Puseyism, or Tractarianism, was a late arrival in Evangelical Hull, but Dikes saw it on visits to his native Ipswich, 'like smoke from a bottomless pit, which threatened to shed darkness over the whole land,' and he feared it would prevail.[30]

Dikes was not a political priest, but religion, politics, morality and the ordering of society were for him a seamless robe. Apart from religion, disaster awaited individual and nation in this world and the next. So he continued to urge 'the advantages of our National Establishment,' and the duty of the ministers of the Church 'to enforce her holy doctrines'.[31]

After the defeat of Napoleon it seemed that England might have escaped the worst effects of revolution, but preaching in 1820, Dikes deplored certain developments in the growing manufacturing towns where there was, he said, 'a growing revolutionary spirit . . . which led to blasphemous assaults on religion'.[32] Ten years later, however, his natural hopefulness asserted itself, even when concessions had been granted to Catholics and farm labourers were burning ricks and smashing machinery in many parts of the country. Even the worst terrors of the French Revolution, he reminded himself, had 'yielded to the influence of time, and the voice of despair was exchanged for notes of praise and thanksgiving to God'.[33] There were Chartist agitations in Hull during Dikes's time, but he always felt that Socialism was more insidious, fearing the effects of 'error covertly insinuated.' In all he remained a pre-revolutionary man to the end of his days. All men were ultimately equal before God, but hierarchy and inequality were necessary in this life for the sake of social order, and Dikes believed that the Established Church had a God-given part to perform in maintaining order.

The gentle Dikes appeared more at ease with the world than Milner, but he was equally unworldly at heart. He reminded a mother who asked advice on training her children that 'the great end of life is to prepare for death,' and that the comforts which God provides must be enjoyed 'with great moderation and great caution'.[34] He spoke, like Milner, of a world full of snares and vanities which all too easily attracted the young. Towards the end of his life he even wondered if he had not himself 'indulged too high expectation from the things of this world . . . an undue love of present objects'.[35] Milner denounced outright the fatal distractions of mercantile life. Dikes contrasted the avid busyness of people in this world with their unreadiness for the next.

His biographer sums up his Evangelical vision of the godly city.

Where ever the stream of divine revelation has flowed, it has gladdened the region through which it has passed; and on its banks have arisen the Sacred Temple, the Sunday and Daily School, the Infirmary, the Almshouse, and the Philanthropic Institution which opens its hospitable door to the blind and the poor, to the old and the wretched.[36]

It is an attractive picture of a godly city with churches for worship and instruction in the faith, schools to teach the children the faith and knowledge 'suitable to their station in life,' and institutions to alleviate the condition of those who through poverty, sickness or old age could no longer keep up. If adapted to modern social conditions, Dikes's vision remains apposite when separated from overtones of a past golden era, but if this idyll ever existed it was beyond recall after two great revolutions. The French Revolution unleashed new aspirations which would not be gainsaid. The effects of the commercial and industrial revolution which Milner hated and which Dikes benignly attempted to enlist on his side, created populations, cities and problems beyond the scope of either the Established Church or an unreformed government and parliament.

Dikes died in 1847 at the house of his old friend Avison Terry, Evangelical merchant and philanthropist, collaborator in building churches and sometime Mayor of Hull. His funeral was attended by clergy, Dissenting ministers, the Mayor and Corporation, twelve magistrates, the Town Clerk, bankers and merchants. Dikes's civilized, courteous brand of Evangelicalism had become the religion which the leading citizens of the day respected, even if many were not the conscientious church-goers he would have liked them to be.

III

Religious Dissent

A 'Dissenter' was any one who departed from the doctrine and practice of the Established Church. Hull's Dissenters, mostly Independents, represented a second strand of Evangelicalism in the later years of the eighteenth century. They were of similar social standing to Anglicans and were to be found in the professions and among the rising commercial classes, merchants and manufacturers. Almost half the Aldermen, Councillors and Magistrates on the new Town Council elected after the Municipal Corporations Act of 1835 were Dissenters, including William Sissons, John Blundell and James Alderson, physician at Hull Royal Infirmary.[1]

Men like these had authority to appoint the minister of their own church and were unlikely to subject themselves to the brand of anti-commercial onslaught which Milner regularly delivered from Holy Trinity pulpit. Politically they were conservative, but religious dissenters against the exclusive privileges of the Established Church. Their brief enthusiasm for the changes taking place in revolutionary Europe raised the suspicions of Churchmen, who soon came to regard Dissent as tantamount to republicanism. Revolution or even major reforms were not in Dissenters' best interests, nor consistent with their social and commercial aspirations. They believed in a balanced constitution, but at the same time they were aware of the need for political and social reform to relieve the poverty in industrial towns.[2]

The oldest Dissenting congregations in Hull were two groups of Puritans in Dagger Lane and Bowlalley Lane which became Unitarian. As a consequence, eleven members left Dagger Lane and built a new chapel in Blanket Row in 1769. George Lambert, a recently trained student of the Dissenting Academy at Heckmondwike, was called to be their minister. He was a man over medium height, broad and full-set with ruddy cheeks and shrewd, bright grey eyes. A lady who knew him in old age remembered his wig and three-cornered hat, dark blue coat, silver buckles, black silk stockings and black small clothes.[3] He was not unlike Joseph Milner in appearance, heavy jowled and bewigged in preaching gown and bands. The two men were to spend the rest of their lives in Hull. While Milner laid the foundations of Evangelicalism in the Church of England, Lambert began to revive Dissent in Hull, which in all parts of England was inward looking, limited to its own conventicles, respectable, self-contained and showing little interest in the world outside.

The practice of Dissenting religion was a simple affair before the nineteenth-century proliferation of church activities and societies. At Blanket Row, apart from Sunday services, there was a Monday prayer meeting and a fortnightly lecture or meeting, so there was plenty of time for Dissenters who wanted to play a full part in the development of the seaport. Lambert's flock, which he visited regularly, was only about twenty strong at first. Some wits at Holy Trinity scoffed at 'that poor devil Lambert who had to preach twice a week to the same people'.[4] It does not follow that Lambert's people were poor. There was little direct contact between the lowest classes and any religious body in Hull. Pew rents were one long-lasting obstacle.[5] Nevertheless, when a new and larger chapel, opened in Fish Street in 1792, was enlarged in 1802 over a thousand people attended the re-opening. It was to remain the centre of Congregationalism in Hull for over a hundred years.

Lambert was at one with Milner in the fight against irreligion, but he also desired religious freedom.[6] Although 'pure religion' was a common bond between Churchmen and the new outward-looking Dissenter, a barrier grew between them. One side stood firmly for the Establishment while the other was increasingly attracted by religious democracy. Lambert was politically a conservative constitutionalist and recorded in his diary his sorrow over the riots and destruction of Dissenters' property in many parts of the country in 1791. The howls of 'Church and King' or 'Church and Constitution' implied that Dissent was inimical to both. The outbreak of war with France made matters even worse.

The friendship between Lambert and the Evangelical clergy in the Established Church outlived these alarms. He had spoken warmly of John King, vicar of St Mary's, Lowgate, on his death in 1782 and when Milner died in 1797 he wrote that 'he was a man of learning and piety, a sound and faithful Gospel minister, and much owned of God in the conversion of souls'.[7] As late as 1816, Mrs Gilbert, the wife of Lambert's successor said that when she came to Hull, 'it was like joining an informal Evangelical Alliance.'

Friendships like these help to explain why Hull's Dissenters were not more openly critical of the Church of England. Lambert confided many thoughts to his diary which he did not care to express publicly. At the turn of the century he attended a Confirmation service in Holy Trinity and did not find it an edifying experience.

Many were asked no questions; others have been confirmed twice the same day; some have offered their tickets to another; many young men come from the country, I saw with common prostitutes; some were drunk. I have read over the prayer-book service, and if I had not been a Dissenter, I should have been one that night. Yet the bishop tells me they have been regenerated, and assures them of God's favour.[8]

Hull's Dissenters tempered any public criticism of abuses within the Church of England, partly through fear of persecution and partly out of regard for their Evangelical friends.

The Establishment was alarmed at the success of Dissent. 1,118 Dissenting chapels in England and Wales in 1776 had increased to 2,000 by 1808. By 1811 in towns with over 1,000 inhabitants there were 3,457 Dissenting chapels to 2,655 Established churches.[9] When in 1809 the Home Secretary, Lord Sidmouth, required returns of all chapels and preachers licensed in the previous fifty years, the figures of 12,000 chapels and 4,000 preachers increased the ruling class's mistrust of Dissent. In his notorious Bill of 1811, Sidmouth promised to save Dissenters from the erstwhile 'pig drovers, chimney sweeps, and tailors' who preached in rural areas. The Bill proposed that no minister could be appointed to a congregation unless he were already well-known to six of their number, and no student could go to college unless six ministers who knew him well testified to his suitableness. If this had become law, the scattered nature of Dissent would have ensured its demise.

The threatening nature of the Bill provoked a mass protest meeting of Hull's Dissenters in Fish Street chapel, chaired by the Revd George Lambert. It was fully reported in a local weekly newspaper, the *Hull Rockingham*, whose editor was George Lee, a Unitarian minister in the town.[10] Every speaker declared his political loyalty. William Severn, once a Wesleyan, now Unitarian minister of Bowlalley Lane chapel, said that Sidmouth's Bill was not motivated by the occasional abuse of the Toleration Act, but by 'the amazing increase of Dissenters within the last thirty or forty years,' not least by Methodists who now counted themselves as Dissenters, he asserted.[11]

The Revd George Payne, Lambert's assistant, said that Dissenters were just as good subjects of the Government as their episcopalian brothers. The law should not require uniformity of belief, but this Bill would exact punishment on those whose creed differed from that of the majority.[12] Others were at pains to make it clear that Dissenters in Hull were all conservatives and that religious Dissent was compatible with political conformity. Look how they had supported the accession of William III, they said, and were among the first to welcome George I. They had remained patient for thirty years since applying for the repeal of the Test and Corporation Acts, but this Bill, if it became law, would make matters worse.[13]

A few days after the meeting in Hull, Sidmouth's Bill was defeated in the House of Lords, but within a year George Payne detected a reviving spirit of intolerance towards Dissenters.[14] The precariousness of religious liberty was one reason why Fish Street Chapel confined its evangelistic work to the remote rural area of Holderness. It might have been argued that extra religious accommodation was required in a town of 27,502 people,[15] but Dissenters in Hull and other towns were still wary of the mob.

Mrs Gilbert, the wife of Fish Street's second minister, attended a large social gathering in 1817. The discussion got deep into 'Manchester politics', a topic of great interest to Dissenting businessmen, so Hull's Dissenters were obliged to sing a chorus of 'God save the King', at the behest of their 'dear Low Church friends' (from St Mary's, Lowgate), who had grown suspicious of their loyalty as the evening continued. If they had declined, their 'friends' would have reported them to the magistrates.[16] Mrs Gilbert had misjudged the limited nature of Hull's 'informal Evangelical Alliance.' The religious congruity of the two strands was not proof against the corrosion of political incompatibility.

During the next twenty years the political climate became more favourable towards Dissenters. The experience of the 'Peterloo Massacre' at Manchester in 1819, a provocative show of force by the magistrates at a non-revolutionary working-class gathering, including women and children, pushed middle and working-class Reformers into each others arms. Dissenters on the whole identified themselves with the Whig policy of defending Queen Caroline at the time of the Queen's trial in 1820, and the repeal of the Test and Corporation Acts in 1828, followed by Catholic Emancipation in 1829, were bitter blows for the Establishment.

The Revd George Lee and other middle-class Dissenters supported moderate Reform Associations rather than the extreme Reform Unions like that set up in Hull by the agitator James Acland, an out-and-out radical and self-selected champion of popular liberty, who arrived from Bristol in 1820.[17] Well-to-do Dissenters like Sissons, Blundell and James Alderson did not claim eligibility for public office simply on the grounds that they were citizens; they believed that the privileges open to men of their class, wealth and station should not be denied them on the grounds of their faith.[18] For them Emancipation was more important than Reform, but Emancipation which began the break up of the old order made Reform inevitable.[19] The fall of the Tory administration in 1830 and the Reform Act of 1832, with the enfranchisement of the entrepreneurial middle class, marked the end of the old order. The long decline of the Church of England in Hull in relation to Dissent also began in the early 1830s and a memorable public dispute between the two in 1834 shows how matters stood. The lead was taken by the Independents, by then moving from a loose federation towards a religious denomination.[20]

The occasion of the dispute, known as 'The Hull Ecclesiastical Controversy,' was the Dissenters' claim that they exerted a greater influence on the life of the town than the Established Church. The leading character on the Dissenting side was the Revd Thomas Stratten, the recently arrived minister of Fish Street chapel, a heavily-built man with an impish look and a quick mind which he soon put to good use. George Lambert, his predecessor, had given most of his attention to Fish Street's Holderness mission; Stratten changed the emphasis towards work within the church, to the young, and to evangelism within the immediate neighbourhood of the chapel. With his philanthropic outlook he took account of people's physical and temporal welfare and created many religious agencies for this purpose. Lambert had little interest in the world outside; Stratten, no less diligent as a pastor, was concerned with the affairs of mankind at large and with the rightful place of Dissent in the modern world.[21]

Hull's Dissenters, as part of a nation-wide Dissenting protest, prepared a petition to Parliament asking for five grievances to be redressed:

(i)   the granting of legal and civil registration of births, marriages and deaths,

(ii)   freedom to celebrate marriages without interference from the episcopal clergy or payment of fees to them,

(iii) complete exemption from church rates,

(iv)   liberty for Dissenting ministers to inter in the national burial grounds,

(v)   the revision of the charters of Oxford and Cambridge Universities in order to abolish the Established Church's monopoly of academic honours, and the establishment of the Universities of London and Durham on liberal and comprehensive principles.

A public meeting in Fish Street Chapel to gather support for the petition was chaired by William Lowthrop, later Mayor of Hull, the only Dissenting landowner active in Hull politics.[22] Over 1,100 attended the meeting, some standing in the aisles and all 'highly respectable, a considerable proportion being ladies'.[23]

No Church of England clergy attended, needless to say, nor were any Wesleyan ministers present. The latter belonged to the largest Dissenting body in Hull which was by this time approaching in numbers the combined total of all other Nonconformists. They were socially confident in their Toryism, not seeking concessions nor wanting to offend their Church of England friends. It was a new Whig member of Parliament, Matthew Hill the barrister, who drew attention to the greater success of Dissent compared with the Established Church in Hull. In the last thirty years, he said, Dissenters had spent twice as much money on places of worship, had almost twice the amount of seating and twice the number of attenders. The number of Sunday School children was double that in the Church of England, and there were six times as many communicants.[24]

The publication of a report of the public meeting stung the clergy of the Established Church into response. They took particular offence at the offer of 'forgiveness' from Dissenters and at being called 'religious functionaries,' and they could not comprehend why Dissenters should feel themselves inferior and proscribed. They would soon understand, wrote Stratten in his subsequent *Review of the Hull Ecclesiastical Controversy*, if they had rates levied on them for repairs to Dissenting buildings, or if they had to go to Dissenting chapels to celebrate marriages or employ the Dissenting minister at burials.[25]

The liberty sought by Hull's Dissenters was for men only. The 'considerable number' of women at Fish Street chapel that night were gently told by Stratten that they were not eligible to sign the petition. Their job was to influence their husbands at home.[26]

The controversy revealed the inability of either Church of England clergy or Dissenting ministers to appreciate their opponents' point of view. The three leading Evangelical clergy in the town, John Scott of St Mary's, Lowgate who died later in the same year, Thomas Dikes of St John's, and John King, the first vicar of Christ Church, wrote a series of 'Clerical Tracts' in reply to the Dissenters' claims. Stratten's *Review* reflects their tone of superiority combined with a deep underlying fear of Dissent. One writer (they did not sign the Tracts individually) saw in the Dissenters' case 'the ebullitions of a mind frenzied by the Revolutionary principles of France.' Another Tract compares Dissenters to 'the rabble which seized Christ and led him away to be crucified', and works in yet more references to the 'base-born principles' of the French Revolution.[27]

Stratten admitted the claim of increased piety in the Established Church, a result of the Evangelical Revival, but increased piety should result in increased justice towards men, especially one's Christian brethren. He poked fun at one writer's plea that Dissenters had been well trained in the use of argument and sophistry, whereas Churchmen had been left to a great degree ignorant of the ground on which their case was vindicated. Was this, asked Stratten, the result of all those privileges which had worked so long to the exclusive benefit of the State Church: the monopoly of the Universities, the public endowments, the labours of the Christian Knowledge Society? Had all this failed to inform Churchmen of the true grounds of their much vaunted system while Dissenters, excluded and proscribed, had been well trained?[28]

Matthew Hill, the Dissenting barrister, suggested a practical test to settle the matter of whether Church or Dissent had the greater influence on Hull's people. The outcome was the census of Church and Chapel Attendances in Hull, 1834 (Appendix 1). In terms of number of buildings, sittings, attendances, communicants and Sunday School children, Dissent outshone the Established Church by a ratio of three to one on almost all counts. Instead of becoming partners at a time when religious denominations were struggling to keep their heads above water in a rising population and an expanding town, Church and Dissent in Hull remained grudging opponents. Their mutual respect was already turning into enmity by the 1830s.

IV

Methodism: from Church to Dissent

Methodism was first brought to Hull by Elizabeth Blow, the wife of a Grimsby shoemaker. She used to cross the river Humber by the market boat and call regularly on her friends Mr and Mrs Midforth in the Ropery, later Humber Street, where a tiny Methodist Society was founded in 1746. Thus Methodism was planted in Hull by a small group of artisans and their wives, and Elizabeth Blow returned to Grimsby 'to sow the seed in other fields'.[1]

A few of the Midforth's neighbours began to meet with them for reading and prayer, but their meetings soon excited the 'scorn and hostility of the ungodly multitude.' One evening, the house was besieged by a large mob which so put the Methodists in fear of their lives that they were obliged to remain indoors until morning. The mob later excused its outrage on the grounds that the Methodists were plotting on behalf of the Pretender to the throne. The Bench dismissed the case when the Bible and the Church Homilies, the alleged sources of subversion, were brought in evidence.[2]

Among those at the Midforth's house that night was Mrs Mary Thompson whose niece Sarah Teal (later Snowden) lived with her. Sarah was almost one hundred years old when she died; she left no journal, but a memoir of her published in 1837 provides a direct link with the beginning of Methodism in Hull.[3] She was also its earliest recorded convert, aged fifteen at the time.

Dramatic conversions, often accompanied by an exaggerated notion of past sins, were usual in Evangelical circles. Sarah Teal's aunt provided lodgings for Hull's first itinerant preachers and Sarah never forgot 'Mr Johnson of York and Mr Hampson'. She also had good cause to remember Mr Hetherington the cabinet maker, Hull's first local preacher, at whose evening service she was converted. When Hetherington prayed aloud that God would 'in that hour bring some poor sinner to himself', Sarah responded, 'O let it be me!' Her life was doubtless relatively innocent before her conversion but she was, she claimed, 'admonished of the sinfulness of her beloved amusements'.[4]

John Wesley's reception on his first visit to Hull in April 1752 was similar to the experience of the little group at the Midforth's house six years before, but on a larger scale and more violent.[5] The quay where he landed was swarming with people who stared, laughed and enquired which was Wesley. Perhaps the Baltic trade was still slack after the winter and the crowd of sight-seers, waiting to identify him, was the mob sizing up its quarry for the night. Wesley, however, walked through them without harm to his host's house in the Market Place, and attended prayers in Holy Trinity at three o'clock.

It was a different scene at six o'clock on the barren stretch of land outside the town wall. The 'huge multitude' was drawn from every level of society, 'rich and poor, horse and foot, with several coaches.' Hull and Sculcoates population was then about 12,000. The hooligan element pelted him with clods and stones and the violence might have proved fatal for Wesley and his wife, who accompanied him. Their coachman had retired to a safe distance leaving them stranded, but fortunately a gentlewoman gave them refuge in her coach. Wesley was a man of slight build but the gentlewoman was of generous proportions, so shielded by her he escaped unharmed, pursued later to his lodging by the mob who broke the windows four stories high. Calm descended about midnight after a final charge on the house and Wesley slept until almost four in the morning. An hour later he and his party left Hull for Pocklington; he needed strong persuasion to visit Hull a second time seven years later. The young Sarah Teal, by then Sarah Snowden, remarked, 'Mr Wesley appears to have considered the soil very unpromising'.[6]

Such unprovoked violence seems remarkable, but as there was no effective police force at the time, the mob performed the dual task of social protest and social control. Methodism was feared by the clergy and gentry as a challenge to public order and to the authority of their class.[7] One did not necessarily need to hire the mob, it acted as it pleased; but to be on the side of the clergy and gentry, to defend Church and Establishment was good enough excuse to indulge in high-spirited hooliganism and religious xenophobia. In a drab life, the diversion itself was as attractive as the cause it claimed to support. From a Methodist point of view, the mob was living proof of the Evangelical doctrine of human depravity.[8]

Methodism began to expand in 1760 with the opening of its first preaching house in the old tower of the ruined Suffolk Palace, opposite St Mary's Church. Hull became the centre of a Circuit in 1771 and a new chapel, replacing the old meeting house, was opened in Manor Alley the following year. By 1774 it could not contain the congregation. 'How this town has changed since I preached on the Carr', said Wesley.[9] On a visit in 1786, Wesley preached in Holy Trinity at the invitation of its first Evangelical incumbent, Arthur Clarke, Wilberforce's brother-in-law; Evangelicals were becoming more acceptable after Milner's years of ostracism. The same year another advance was made with the arrival of Joseph Benson, the new superintendent Methodist minister. Before he came there was rarely more than 200 in the congregation; within a very short time Manor Alley was full to overflowing and plans were launched to build a second chapel in George Yard. On its completion Wesley described it as 'nearly as large as the new chapel in London'.[10]

When Wesley was next invited to preach in Holy Trinity he dined afterwards at the vicarage. Although nearing the end of his life, he was still at the height of his powers and now completely acceptable to the Established Church in Hull; secession was unthinkable while he lived. In spite of his irregular practices, he was the major figure in England's Evangelical revival and the withdrawal of his followers from the Church of England so soon after his death was a tragedy not only for Evangelicals. Wesley was a popular and acceptable figure in his last days, but Methodists in general were not. On his last visit to Hull he wrote to Bishop Pretyman of Lincoln complaining of the persecution of Methodists. Wesley's preachers and people were still members of the Established Church, but to ensure their own survival, chapels and preachers in many parts of the country obtained licences under the Toleration Act; thus they were obliged to declare themselves Dissenters against their will.[11]

Between Wesley's death in 1791 and the end of the century, two important events occurred, one of national, the other of local importance. Methodism split nationally, but there was a remarkable growth in membership of the Hull Circuit. Within a month of Wesley's death nine preachers from Halifax sent out a circular letter saying that Methodists in future should be governed by the Conference Plan and form themselves into committees. Methodist government was to be conciliar rather than monarchic.[12] All preachers had to submit to Wesley's control while he lived, but they were unlikely to afford the same allegiance to another leader.

The 1791 Conference agreed to follow the plan left by Wesley, but an ambiguity remained over the Connexion's relationship with the Established Church. Those who called themselves Church Methodists did not want to separate, but some, while not wanting a formal break, recognised that Methodism was inevitably developing a life of its own, not least because of its founder's own actions and pragmatic approach to evangelism. Many Methodists in Hull still received Holy Communion from, and valued their relationship with, Churchmen like Milner, Clarke and Dikes and urged that Methodists should not profess themselves Dissenters, nor meet for worship in Church hours. They feared that if Methodism seceded from the Church of England, it would 'dwindle away into a dry, dull, separate party'.[13] Worshippers at George Yard Chapel agreed not to open the chapel during Church services 'in accord with Mr Wesley's wishes.'

Methodist itinerant preachers, never spending more than a few years in one post, had little time to absorb local feelings. In any case many came directly into Methodism with no experience of the Established Church, so could not be expected to show any great loyalty to it. Thomas Taylor, a Hull preacher, believed it was perfectly in order for him to administer Holy Communion to his people who had lived so long without it.[14] Alexander Kilham, born at Epworth and accepted as a preacher by Wesley in 1785, felt an even greater antipathy towards the Church. He pointed out that many Methodists never received Holy Communion because they could not in conscience take it from ungodly ministers in the company of unworthy communicants in their parish church; others received the sacrament in Dissenting chapels for the same reason.[15]

John Pawson, who first experienced Methodism as a young man when lodging in Hull, became increasingly critical of Wesley's one-man leadership and advocated separation from the Church. He was aware of a widening gulf between ministers and trustees and the aspirations of ordinary people.

Trustees, he said, were usually the richest and most powerful men in the Connexion, but not the most pious, lively or zealous, so it might be best for powers of decision to be shared among the majority.[16] Kilham, in language reminiscent of revolutionary France, said it was a form of tyranny and oppression for Conference to decide on hours of service and the administration of the sacrament. He alarmed not only the Establishment, but also his former friends in Methodism to whom he now seemed no better than a Jacobin or a follower of Thomas Paine. They cast aspersions on his character and on his conduct as a preacher. During the 1797 Conference he met with three other preachers to form what later became the Methodist New Connexion.[17] Its followers met with scant success in Hull compared with the main strands of Methodism, Wesleyan and, later, Primitive, although a New Connexion chapel was built in North Street in 1798.

There were some in Hull who felt that Methodism was moving too far from the Church of England. They also withdrew from the local Society and set up in a building in Osborne Street where they continued to hold services out of Church hours and remained on friendly terms with the Church of England for many years.[18] At the 1851 Census there were almost twice as many of these Church (or Independent) Methodists at public worship as in the New Connexion.

The strife and division of the 1790s did not inhibit Methodism's expansion; on the contrary it was a period of unprecedented growth in the Hull Circuit. The reasons are complex and the evidence confusing; Methodists at the time attributed it simply to energetic preaching and providential intervention.

There was a 'rising tide'[19] in Methodism in a number of northern towns. Hull's *annus mirabilis*, according to Richard Treffrey, was 1794.[20] Over a period of twenty-two years, Methodist membership had increased by an aggregate of thirty-two members, but in 1794 it shot up from 640 to 1,280.

Treffrey wrote, 'the Lord sent a gracious rain upon his inheritance; the work which had been nearly stationary for so long a time, was now gloriously revived'.[21]

A modern historian, W.R. Ward, believes that the 'evangelical torrent' in the mid-1790s was not the result of urban Jacobinism, but of the subsistence crisis of 1795.[22] Although the *annus mirabilis* in Hull had been 1794, there were food riots in Hull in 1795 and 1796, started by women and boys on the verge of starvation when the price of flour rose.[23] How far this affected the growth of Hull Methodism is difficult to judge; Hull was a commercial town where non-established religion flourished and the Church of England had already begun its long decline in the face of industrial and political revolution.[24] The years 1794, 1797, 1804 and 1814 were for Sarah Snowden, 'times of rejoicing, as they were distinguished by the unusual prosperity of Jerusalem which she loved'.[25] Superintendent minister Joseph Benson's daughter, Ann, was eleven years old when her father began his second spell in Hull in 1797. She remembered it as a time of great movement 'among religious people.' There were many revival meetings which were for Ann an 'incitement to a life of piety'.[26]

Other local statistical evidence, however, throws some doubt both on Treffrey's and on the Minutes of Conference figures for late eighteenth-century and early nineteenth-century Hull. A Hull Circuit Stewards' Book, 1806-1833, survived at least until the early years of the twentieth century,[27] and records annual membership numbers from 1793 onwards. The table shows similar proportional increases around the year 1795, but the aggregates are only about half Treffrey's 1,280. It is possible that owing to the frequent redrawing of circuit boundaries as Methodism increased, the Minutes of Conference figures for Hull include many from outside the Circuit.

Whatever may have been the exact numbers of Methodists in Hull and district at the beginning of the nineteenth century, they were a significant advance on the 'little flock' whom

Wesley returned to visit in 1759. If the peak membership figure in the Circuit Stewards' Book, 785 in 1796, is trebled to allow for adherents, Methodism was influential among about ten per cent of Hull's people.

Primitive Methodism, like the New Connexion, was the result of a dissension with the main Wesleyan body. Its founders were Hugh Bourne, a carpenter and William Clowes, a potter. The latter was born at Burslem in 1780 and worked in Hull in his unregenerate days, unaffected by the rising influence of Methodism. He fled to his native Staffordshire to escape the clutches of the Press Gang after a drunken brawl outside the Dock and Duck in High Street,[28] and arrived home in the middle of a religious revival. He soon became a tract distributor and class leader, appearing on a circuit plan as an 'exhorter'.[29] He and Bourne were expelled in 1810 for joining in camp meetings which the Wesleyan Conference considered 'highly improper and likely to be of considerable mischief'.[30] So Primitive Methodism was born in 1811. The new movement was a resurgence like the first days of Methodism itself, but the uninhibited enthusiasm of its field meetings, its preachings and long hours of vociferous prayer were not to the taste of the dignified, orderly ways of nineteenth-century Wesleyans.

A group of women was instrumental in bringing Primitive Methodism to Hull. Among them was Hannah Woolhouse, a Wesleyan class leader who had aspirations to preach. In this she was encouraged by her husband, a sack and sailcloth manufacturer, but it was an ambition frowned upon by the Wesleyan Connexion. Hannah Woolhouse and another woman visited Nottingham in 1817 and joined enthusiastically in a revival there before returning to Hull to publicize the exciting new movement in Methodism. In December 1818 Woolhouse again visited Nottingham and appeared at the quarterly meeting to request that the Primitive Methodists send a preacher to Hull.[31]

Clowes arrived in 1819 and in contrast with the quiet, almost secret arrival of Methodism at the Midforth's house in 1746, preached twice in public on the day of his arrival, once in an old foundry, where he found two classes waiting for his arrival, and once in the open, before setting off on his first tour of seven villages to the west of the town where would-be Primitive Methodists were ready to be organized into societies. Within nine months Mill Street (later West Street) chapel was built at a cost of £2,000.[32] Membership increased from 402 to 856 by the end of the year and Hull became the centre of a fourth Primitive Methodist Circuit with three travelling preachers and 900 members.

The Connexion pushed north along the Yorkshire coast, west to Leeds and over the Pennines to Cumberland and Westmorland. By 1824 seventeen Circuits were created from Hull with a membership of 7,660. Total Primitive Methodist membership in England grew from 7,842 to 33,507 in the same period[33] and Hull was the base for missionary journeys from Newcastle to the south coast. Mission stations in London and from Kent to Cornwall were all under the jurisdiction of the Hull Quarterly Board until taken over by the General Missionary Council in 1843. For twenty-three years Hull was the 'Metropolis of Primitive Methodism'.[34]

A distinctive Evangelical fervour was especially noticeable in the long hours devoted to worship by Primitive Methodists. Services began on a Saturday evening, and there might be four or five on Sunday, beginning at six o'clock in the morning and ending after nine o'clock in the evening. But unlike the 'little flock' of the 1740s and 1750s, Primitive Methodists were not obliged to meet in secret behind locked doors for fear of the mob. They met boldly out of doors, and Hull was agreeably surprised at their good order and respectability. A farmer might lend his field on a Sunday for a camp meeting at which several thousands gathered from nine o'clock in the morning

until four in the afternoon, without any misbehaviour, listening
to a series of sermons preached from a farm wagon.[35]

Hull had four 'spacious' Primitive Methodist chapels by
mid-century[36] capable of accommodating 4,000. Membership
was over 1,500. William Clowes died in Hull in 1851. His last
public engagement was a meeting in Mason Street Chapel to
plan for a new chapel in Jarratt Street[37] which became the
Clowes' Memorial chapel.

If Dissent spanned middle and upper classes then
Methodism's social spectrum was Dissent's mirror image,
linking the middle and lower classes but concentrating its
energies on the poor. Three-quarters of all early Methodists in
England were manual workers, but the unskilled were heavily
outnumbered by artisans. Victorian Wesleyanism was not so
bourgeois as popularly thought. Before 1850 the majority were
in broadly artisan occupations (type 'E' Appendix II), and
when the artisan class lost its overall supremacy in Methodism
generally it still remained ahead of the lower middle-class
group. Primitive Methodists also became more respectable over
the years, but throughout the nineteenth century 80 per cent of
Primitive Methodists were manual workers, although more
likely to be semi-skilled workers or craftsmen than labourers.

The upward mobility of Methodists contrasts with the
working-class movement of Wesley's time,[38] but the
discontinuity was not so marked in Hull where the founding
members were very respectable artisans and shopkeepers.
Joseph Gee, a hosier from Nottingham who moved to Hull to
continue his business in High Street in 1787, rebuked two ladies
in his shop for complaining that 'Methodism was so much
identified with the poor'.[39] The ladies saw themselves as
members of a middle-class congregation doing good among the
poor. Joseph Spence, the ironmonger who attended the opening
of George Yard Chapel, and Thomas Thompson, the banker
and first Methodist MP, were both local preachers. The majority
of the Trustees at George Yard were among the comfortably-off,

including William Kelsey, broker, John Harrop, dock surveyor, Joseph Cockerill, shipowner, Richard Wade, raff merchant, and William Ramsden, stationer and tea-dealer. Sarah Snowden moved up in the world when she became the superintendent at her son Benjamin's Mercantile Academy in Blanket Row in 1789, the longest-lived private school in Hull.

Thirty Primitive Methodist classes in 1851 which met at addresses in poor areas of the town, Dryden's Entry, Paradise Row, Bethel Place, and the like, had fallen to twenty-five by 1856. Even Primitive Methodists were finding it difficult to survive in such areas. The Methodist New Connexion chapel, Bethel in Charlotte Street, had 184 members at the end of the century. Typical occupations were clerk, hairdresser, pattern maker, insurance agent, watchmaker, shopkeeper and foreman. There was a caretaker, possibly the chapel caretaker, and one dentist.[40]

Of twenty-two marriages at Kingston Wesleyan Chapel in 1846-48, there was one labourer and one 'gentleman' son of a labourer. Apart from a Wesleyan minister whose father was a publisher, the remainder were of the artisan class, joiners, plumbers, drapers, grocers, etc. The bride's occupation, when recorded, reflects women's employment opportunities in the 1840s. She was usually a milliner, dressmaker or staymaker, occasionally a domestic servant.[41]

In 1881 there were over 135 baptisms at Hessle Road Primitive Methodist Chapel, an area which had expanded rapidly in the previous ten years, where most inhabitants were connected with the fishing industry. Twenty-five labourers, or more likely their wives, still looked to the Primitive Methodist chapel as the place to take their infant. The parents of the other ninety, if they were not fishermen, were barmen, joiners, fitters, clerks, platelayers or bricklayers. One father was a smack owner.[42]

By the turn of the century the Marriage Registers of Wesleyan and Primitive Methodists are remarkably similar. The names of small businessmen may be found in both, as well as everything from farm labourers to school teachers, but the occasional solicitor, draughtsman, or the daughter of a silk mercer always married in the Wesleyan chapel.[43]

The large, and often striking Wesleyan chapels were chiefly responsible for giving Hull the outward appearance of a typical northern Nonconformist town, although the George Yard Chapel of which Wesley was so proud was a plain brick building. In the nineteenth century, as wealth increased, Doric pillars began to appear, supporting front porticos. Kingston Chapel in Witham was the largest, able to seat 2,000 worshippers. The most splendid chapel of all, opened in Great Thornton Street in 1842, had a magnificent portico supported by a line of eight fluted pillars thirty feet high and three feet in diameter, with Corinthian capitals. There were two wings, connected by open arcades with two lines of pillars supporting their roofs. The frontage, 160 feet in length with a portico sixty-six feet wide, was approached by an impressive flight of steps. A well-known contemporary print shows a crinolined and top-hatted after-church parade in front of this tremendous reminder of the glories of Greece. It is a picture of Wesleyan Methodist merchants and their wives in their mid-nineteenth century pomp.

This chapel, one of Hull's outstanding buildings, was largely destroyed by fire in 1907.[44] Classical buildings set Nonconformity apart from the Church of England with its more traditional designs. The first Wesleyan chapel in a Gothic style, Beverley Road Chapel, was opened in 1862 and closed in 1941. Lincoln Street Primitive Methodist Chapel, built in 1872 and closed in 1935, was another early example of Nonconformist Gothic.[45]

V

Anti-Catholic Hull

Whatever their religious affiliation, most English people in the eighteenth and nineteenth centuries called themselves Protestants. Catholicism was foreign and un-English, but the monarch's Coronation Oath and the political settlement of 1689 ensured that Catholicism would remain the aberration of a handful of landed gentry and their retainers. Yet in less than a century these cherished bulwarks were no longer proof against Catholic infiltration.

The rising challenge of Catholicism stemmed from the Act of Union in 1800 which merged Ireland with Great Britain, abolished the Irish Parliament and made Westminster directly responsible for Irish affairs. Before the famine of 1840 and the consequent emigration, up to seven million people became the responsibility of the government in London; that five and a half million of them were Roman Catholic inevitably raised fears in the Church of England for the stability of the Establishment with its attendant Anglican privileges. The population of England and Wales in 1831 was just over fourteen million.[1]

Many Dissenters wanted equality of status with the Church of England, and its disestablishment. Roman Catholics were seen as a greater threat by the Established Church than Dissent. They represented an authoritarian, foreign, religio-political power which, given the opportunity, might supplant the Established Church and place a Catholic monarch on England's Protestant throne. The threat was more disturbing since Catholics constituted the large and turbulent majority of the population of Ireland, now part of Great Britain. Through political agitation and religious revival in Ireland and England, Catholics achieved an importance they had not possessed for centuries.

Irish immigrants congregated in London, Liverpool, Birmingham and other large towns where major public works, railways and docks were under construction, but Hull's place on the eastern seaboard, its links with Protestant Europe, its isolation and characteristic industrial economy, attracted a relatively small number of Irish Catholics.

It might have been supposed that Dissenters and the Church of England in Hull, with their close religious affinities, would join forces against the popish threat, but social and political differences prevented any such alliance. Evangelical Tories suspected Dissenters of radicalism. Ironically, Dissenters and Roman Catholics suffered almost equally from discrimination and were put to similar disadvantage by the exclusive privileges, civil, religious and educational to which the Established Church clung so tenaciously.

There were Church leaders in England who saw the relief of Catholic disabilities as a matter of principle, but the Evangelical clergy in Hull, led by the Revd John King, vicar of Christ Church from 1822, were vehemently anti-Catholic and fought their cause on every possible occasion. The *Hull Advertiser* went so far as to accuse them of neglecting their pastoral duties out of an obsession with religious rectitude and sectarian advantage. If Joseph Milner lamented the worldly distractions of the expanding port, his successors were distracted for half a century by sectarian controversy.

The Relief Act of 1778 permitted Catholic worship. A further Act in 1791 removed restrictions on education and marriage and opened most professions to Catholics. The Emancipation Act of 1829, by allowing Catholics to sit in Parliament, brought them within reach of real political power, and thus of influence over the Established Church. Evangelicals, the Corporation and others in Hull were much alarmed, and protest meetings were held and petitions organised at the time the Bill was going through Parliament.

In 1829 the clergy sent a petition to both Houses protesting against further concessions of political power to Roman Catholics.[2] Augustus O'Neil, one of Hull's two MPs, presented two anti-Catholic petitions in the Commons, one from the Mayor and Aldermen, the other purporting to be signed by 3,000 inhabitants, clergy, bankers, merchants and shipowners.[3] Daniel Sykes, Hull's other MP, was in favour of Emancipation on grounds of religious liberty, believing that concessions were necessary to prevent civil disorder and danger to the Established Church. He presented a pro-Catholic petition on behalf of Hull Unitarians and 'other friends of religious liberty'.[4] The Church of England's vehement hostility towards Emancipation was tempered by sympathy for the Catholic predicament on the part of a number of Dissenters. Hull's Unitarians were the natural leaders among Dissenters of this frame of mind, a middle-class intelligentsia, marginalised both by the Established Church and by mainstream Nonconformity. Wesleyan Methodists generally, following the example of John Wesley, were unsympathetic towards Catholics. The *Wesleyan Methodist Magazine* saw Emancipation as 'a dangerous encroachment on Church and State by a people given to rebellion'.[5]

Isaac Wilson, editor and proprietor of the *Hull Advertiser*,[6] a Tory with strong anti-Catholic sentiments, proposed a public meeting to make clear the real wishes of 'the thinking inhabitants of Hull.' Wilson was incensed by Sykes's claim that O'Neil's petition had only a few hundred signatures, rather than 3,000 'in all ranks and professions.' The Revd George Lee, Unitarian editor of the *Hull Rockingham*, backed Sykes and bad feeling developed between the two journals.[7]

The public meeting was held in the Market Place on 2 March 1829, under the shadow of Holy Trinity Church and Peter Scheemaker's equestrian statue of William III, Hull's great symbol of Protestantism. Three hundred were expected, but 5,000 gathered before the meeting began, and this number had swollen to between 8,000 and 10,000 before the end,[8] almost a third of the town's population. The speeches were dominated by the Evangelical clergy, Dikes, Scott of St Mary's, Knight of St James', and King. They were in favour of religious freedom, they said, but Roman Catholics could not be trusted with civil power; they were under foreign influence and had no liberty of their own. John King of Christ Church attacked Sykes and asserted that he would now find all Hull against him. This was not true, but King's oratory drew hisses from the crowd every time he mentioned Sykes's name. When, at last, the Revd Edward Oakes, the Wesleyan minister was allowed to speak, he took the opportunity to assert yet again Methodism's loyalty to the British constitution.

Once Catholic Emancipation became law, Hull settled down to a period of relative calm with sporadic reports of anti-Catholic feeling. Catholics contrasted the bigotry and intolerance of Tories with the liberality of those in Hull who supported Parliamentary and Municipal Reform in 1832 and 1835.[9] An attempt to obstruct freedom of worship for Catholic workhouse children was one example of the many irritants Catholics had to endure.[10] After the Municipal Corporations Act of 1835, three Catholics were elected to the Town Council and were urged to vote for Reform.

Two men arrived on the scene in 1841 who made important contributions to the Evangelical-Catholic debate, this time not on the side of Evangelicalism. Robert Wilberforce, William Wilberforce's son, was appointed Archdeacon of the East Riding and Rector of Burton Agnes. He came from the parish of East Farleigh in Kent. E.F. Collins, a Roman Catholic and philosophic radical came to Hull to edit the *Hull Advertiser*. Wilberforce, much admired by Collins, was a notable example of the off-spring of Evangelical parents who either moved to the Catholic wing of the Church of England or became Roman Catholics. Samuel Wilberforce, Robert's elder brother, was appointed Anglican Bishop of Oxford; John Henry Newman, Henry Manning and Robert Wilberforce, all from Evangelical families, became Roman Catholics. Manning and Newman were to become cardinals, and Robert Wilberforce was to die of fever in Rome in 1857 while preparing for the Catholic priesthood.[11]

Robert Wilberforce was a man of his time in his relations with the lower orders. A Tory paternalist with little sympathy for democracy or Dissenting religion, he found the Yorkshire rural clergy uncouth and difficult to handle.[12] This experience and fears about his Catholic sympathies by the more earnest clergy in Hull were a recipe for bad relations and misunderstandings. It was clear where his sympathies lay as soon as he took up his preferment. His own squire accused him of Tractarianism in 1842, and his charge to the clergy the following year, dealing with the Evangelical and Tractarian movements, made it obvious how matters stood. Wilberforce continued to correspond with Newman and Manning; he had known them at Oriel College, Oxford, and he was encouraged to consider the superiority of Catholicism in letters from his ex-curate, William Henn, who had developed Tractarian sympathies with Wilberforce and was received into the Roman Catholic Church in 1850.[13]

The controversy which led the Archdeacon to secede from the Church of England began in 1854 over a doctrinal matter: the Real Presence in the Eucharist. It was the subject of

Wilberforce's charge to the clergy and he was about to publish a book on the subject. The majority of the Hull clergy took umbrage and signed a letter of protest. They did not have the stomach to take the matter to the ecclesiastical courts, so let things rest once their protest was signed. But the controversy continued to rage week after week in Hull's newspapers, and there was a surprising amount of support for Wilberforce, given the Evangelical ascendancy in the Church in Hull. Even some who did not sympathise with Wilberforce's views wrote to reprimand the clergy for their constant backbiting; it seemed a largely clerical controversy to Collins and the letter-writers to his newspaper.[14] The typical church-goer at the time was female, middle-class, fashionably dressed and always ready to support her vicar's opinions, 'angels arrayed in Parisian bonnets and Polka jackets.' Wilberforce's position became untenable and he sent his resignation to the Archbishop of York on 30 August 1854, becoming a Roman Catholic shortly afterwards. He was about to publish another book, this time on the Royal Supremacy, and could not face another uproar from the Hull clergy.[15]

Collins of the *Advertiser* lamented that the clergy might go on driving people out until no men of learning, piety and zeal were left. The Revd Thomas Bonnin, curate for the long-time absentee vicar of Sculcoates, observed that the Evangelical clergy were really Dissenters inside the Church and would be happier if they joined those outside.[16] The Establishment and their place in an hierarchical society, however, meant so much to Evangelicals that no rapprochement with Dissent was likely.

The restoration of the Catholic hierarchy in England in 1850 provoked a howl of protest from Hull's Evangelical clergy. They demanded a meeting which Robert Wilberforce convened at their request, but declined to attend himself as an advocate of religious tolerance. Fourteen clergy signed a letter to the Queen requesting her to consider the violation of her supremacy by the Papal Bull which created a new Roman

Catholic archiepiscopal see at Westminster.[17] The Archbishop of York, Thomas Musgrove, had no sympathy for Wilberforce's stand and publicly commended those who had signed the address to the Queen.[18]

After 1850 an uneasy feeling was growing in Hull that the Church of England was losing ground against the greater efficiency and zeal of the Church of Rome. This made the visit of Father Alessandro Gavazzi, the ex-Barnabite friar, all the more welcome. He was a friend of Garibaldi, a prolific writer and public speaker who had broken off his allegiance to the papacy.[19] His lecture in Hull's Public Rooms in Jarratt Street in 1856, 'England on the High Road to Popery', sounded just what the Evangelicals wanted, but they were less than pleased when he criticised a proposal to create twelve new Church of England bishoprics which, he said, would be a distraction from real work among the poor. Catholics, he asserted, already did more than the Church of England; because Catholics worked among the poor, so more of the poor became Catholics[20]. His emphasis on the need for working clergy confirmed the fears of those who felt that the Church of England had fallen behind through neglect of the poor in favour of political controversy and a zeal for purity of doctrine.

In the 1850s and 60s, death removed a generation of old adversaries from the scene. Robert Wilberforce, the Tractarian Anglican Archdeacon who became a Roman Catholic, died in 1857. King, the most vehemently out-spoken anti-Catholic in Hull, died in 1858, followed by his lieutenants, Knight in 1862 and Scott in 1865. Anti-Catholic prejudice survived them, of course, but it never again reached the same vituperative heights. Arguably, E.F. Collins' able defence of Catholics in his newspaper and on public platforms helped to prevent prejudice turning into persecution, but he also withdrew from the fray, eventually dying in retirement at Clapham in 1879.[21] He was never a good businessman, and the ownership of the *Advertiser* passed to a limited company in 1851. He continued as editor until 1865 when the paper was incorporated in the *Eastern Morning News*, but in the latter part of his editorship, Collins' attention was given increasingly to non-ecclesiastical affairs, the Dock Company, sanitary reform, the rebuilding of Hull's workhouse, and the establishment of the local board of health.[22] By the 1870s anti-Catholic sentiment in the town had receded almost to the point of indifference, as the notorious 'Hull Convent Case' of 1869 suggests.

Protestant mistrust has always been aroused by the 'religious' life of monks and nuns. There had never been a female convent in Hull, even in pre-Reformation times. All 'religious' in the city at that period were males, monks or friars. It was, therefore, something new for Hull when four novices were received into the Irish Sisterhood of Mercy in St Charles' Church in 1857, to teach in the Catholic girls' schools in Dansom Lane and Canning Street.[23] The *Hull Packet*, Hull's oldest newspaper, and one of strong Protestant convictions, took great exception to the arrival of these 'prurient brides of Christ.' The *Packet* was upset by the vow to remain unmarried and complained of all the pomp and ceremony at their reception, aimed to impress those of Tractarian sympathies.[24] The Hull Convent Case was extraordinary in that it was not the traditional story, beloved of Protestants, in which a young girl is walled up in a convent against her will. In this case a nun had been expelled from the convent.

Susanna Mary Saurin, an Irish-born nun in the Anlaby Road convent, where the Sisterhood had settled, sued the Mother Superior for libel and slander and for conspiring to drive her from the order. Sister Mary Scholastica Joseph, as Mary Saurin was known in the order, claimed she had been falsely accused of a series of negligences before an investigating commission, chaired by the Rt Revd Robert Cornthwaite, Roman Catholic Bishop of Beverley.[25] At the trial, before the Court of the Queen's Bench in Westminster Hall, Sister Mary Joseph, mother superior, referred to as 'Mrs Star', told how

Saurin had been difficult from the time she joined the convent and was recognized by the sisters as the odd one out whom no other order would accept. Her offences were small matters in themselves, eating secretly between meals, borrowing small items from other sisters without their permission, lighting lamps without permission and setting the clock back to cover her lateness for duty. It was alleged that she beat the school children without cause and stole their food. She repeatedly found excuses to talk with externs (people who were not members of the order) and rose early in the morning, again 'without permission,' to go into the garden to look for birds' nests.

For these infringements she was eventually demoted from the convent school and set to work in the laundry. She was, said her counsel, obliged to scrub floors, clean the hearth and do every kind of menial work. On one occasion, as a penance, she was forced to wear a dust cloth over her head (she irritated everybody by wearing it longer than required), on another to apologise for lateness by kissing the floor. In her final seven months at Anlaby Road, after refusing to leave the convent of her own accord, she was restricted to a single room, a bed with too few blankets, and condemned to complete silence. Letters were withheld from her and those she wrote were not forwarded. Her food, in the end the leavings of others, was not fit to eat.

The twenty-day trial was packed with spectators, the majority sympathetic to the plaintiff on account of the treatment she had received. Hundreds were unable to get into the court, and the proceedings were fully reported in *The Times* and the Hull newspapers. *The Times* referred to Mary Saurin as the 'poor lady'.[26]. The jury, however, found in favour of the defendants on the counts of assault and imprisonment, and for the plaintiff on the counts of libel and conspiracy, but reduced damages from the £5,000 claimed to £500, including the dowry of £300 which the convent promised to return. It was virtually a victory for the defendants. Saurin withdrew to a convent in Europe as a parlour boarder and the convent in Anlaby Road continued to develop.

Although the case was reported in great detail, anti-Catholic sentiment in 1869 had lost the virulence of 1828-50. Public interest was beginning to wane by the end of the second week,[27] in spite of one leader writer's attempt to keep it going with a salacious revelation of 'a very serious charge of impropriety of conduct', said to be contained in the written statements of the Bishop of Beverley's Commission of Enquiry. It was alleged that Saurin had habitually tried to attract the attention of Father John Motler, assistant at St Charles' Church, and that becoming greatly excited when he was in the house, she threw herself on her knees beside him and 'asked him to go with her'.[28] Motler was not called to give evidence at the trial and Saurin said she had simply told him on one occasion that lunch was ready.[29]

Comments in Hull were anti-conventual rather than anti-Catholic, ranging from assertions about the 'unnaturalness' of convent life to expressions of satisfaction that the revelations of disorder and uncharitableness proved what people had always suspected.[30] A letter to the editor complained of the suppression of natural affections and that the inmates became tools and chattels of a 'foreign power.' The writer hoped no more convents would be allowed to be built in England,[31] but there was little or no comment apart from that created in the newspapers by themselves. The *Hull Times* said, sneeringly, that although the case merely involved 'women's squabbles' which took up the time of eminent and busy people for almost three weeks, its value lay in the glimpse into convent life, 'which we have long hoped for, but never seen before'.[32] Convents, according to one champion of the Victorian municipal system, should be 'subject to the wholesome and purifying influence of Government inspection'.[33]

The case was soon forgotten; there was little capital to be made from it and interest quickly moved on to other matters:

the introduction of Gladstone's Irish Church Bill with its talk of disestablishment and disendowment.[34] A generation was growing up in Hull to whom Roman Catholics, even if strange and rather foreign, were an acceptable part of the community. The political settlement of 1689 and the threats of 1789, the stuff of life to the Revd John King and his like, meant less to the rising generation. The more recent fears and alarms of 1829 and 1850 were also passing into history.

Another possible reason for the apparent acceptance of Catholicism lay in the town's growing reputation for indifference towards organized religion. Even Catholics were not immune. A series of articles in 1872 in *The Nation*, an Irish nationalist weekly published in London, entitled 'The Irish in England' by Hugh Heinrick, singled out Hull as the town where the largest proportion of Irish were fallen and lost.

> Hull is the only town I have known where whole families have separated themselves in idea and sentiment from their kindred, and, renegades to Faith and Fatherland, have ranged themselves on the side of England and infidelity. The general condition of the town is low, and the condition of the Irish population corresponds with its surroundings.[35]

Heinrick reckoned the Irish population in Hull to be between 5,000 and 6,000, that is between 4 and 5 per cent of the total population. In spite of Heinrick's gloomy outlook, at the Hull Religious Census of 1881 there were 2,414 Catholics attending church on census Sunday (Appendix IV).

The Irish population in Hull may have been 'low' but, for the faithful, an astonishing reminder of the ultramontane triumphalism associated with Cardinal Vaughan's archiepiscopate at Westminster (1892-1903) can still be seen in the interior of St Charles' Church. Many complained of its barnlike baldness when it was opened in 1829, and a number of additions and embellishments were added in 1835. Today's striking and elaborate interior was the work of the local architects Smith, Broderick and Lowther in 1894. They employed the German artist Heinrich Immenkamp, then living in Hull, who transformed the interior into a highly dramatic version of the lavish late Rococo settings in central and southern Germany.[36] Most of the worshippers may have been poor in this world's goods and felt themselves to be part of a minority religious group in Hull, but such magnificent surroundings spoke the language of a confident internationalism. Almost four centuries after their religion was proscribed in England, Catholics were reassured that they belonged to the greatest Church in Christendom.

VI

Going to Church

The urbanization of Hull created great disparities of wealth. Workers were crowded together, hastily and inadequately housed, ignorant, ill-fed, irregularly employed and prone to disease and early death through poverty, bad sanitation and lack of medicine. These conditions were not new, but migration to the industrial towns in search of employment and an escape from rural indigence spawned large urban ghettos of poverty. The rich, on the whole, bore this state of affairs with fortitude, but the Churches and other philanthropic bodies endeavoured to ameliorate the condition of the poor. The Churches, however, believed that their chief responsibility was to provide pews for the growing population and to persuade them to attend religious worship.

Hull's population, approaching 23,000 in 1792, was 32,958 by 1831 in the municipal borough alone.[1] This was chiefly the result of an increasing number of docks. The first three, built on the site of the medieval walls, turned Old Town into an island bounded on the south by the Humber and on the east by the river Hull. New, fashionable streets were built to the north by the merchants and professional classes who moved out of High Street; the more affluent built their mansions further west on the higher ground at Hessle. The first large concentration of working-class housing outside Old Town was in the St James' district, named after the church which Dikes built in his attempt to accommodate its inhabitants.

In 1832 the parliamentary borough comprised Hull town part and the parishes of Sculcoates and Drypool, by then one continuous urban area. At the 1831 census their populations were:-

Hull town part	32,958
Sculcoates parish	13,468
Drypool parish	2,935
Total population	49,361 [2]

In the first thirty years of the century, said the Revd Thomas Stratten (Appendix I), Nonconformists spent twice as much as the Church of England on building and repairing churches, provided twice the number of sittings, had twice as many attendances, communicants and Sunday School children, and almost three times the number of Sunday School teachers.

The Church of England's parish churches, Holy Trinity, St Mary's, Lowgate, St Mary's, Sculcoates and St Peter's, Drypool were supplemented by four 'chapels of ease,' St John's (1792), Christ Church (1822), the Mariners' Church (1828) and St James' (1831). Seven of these, omitting Holy Trinity where the Revd J.H. Bromby was vicar, represented the solid base of Evangelicalism in Hull. Out of 1,000 families in Holy Trinity and St Mary's parishes in the middle of the eighteenth century, only about 100 were Nonconformist, but the increasing labouring and artisan population of the expanding town prepared the ground for the first great advance in Nonconformist influence.

Nonconformists quickly established themselves in the new areas of the town. The Independents built Providence

Chapel in Hope Street (1797), Tabernacle in Sykes Street (1826), Trinity Chapel in Nile Street (1827), a large chapel in Witham (1830) and Salem Chapel in Cogan Street (1832). The Baptists built George Street Chapel in 1796, but Wesleyan Methodism's growth was the most impressive. After the George Yard Chapel in 1786, Wesleyans moved into the newly populated areas to build chapels in Scott Street (1804), Raikes Street (1805), Waltham Street (1826), Alfred Street (1830), returning to Old Town in 1833 to build Humber Street Chapel. Wesleyans also had two large schools in English Street and Mason Street where services were held twice a week.[3] Ten places of worship built within fifty years compared Wesleyan efforts to advantage against the Established Church's eight churches, four of them inherited from the past. Primitive Methodists had two chapels; New Connexion and Church Methodists one each. There was also the Sailors' Chapel, the hull of an old 400-ton ship moored in Prince's Dock, the Nonconformist equivalent of the Mariners' Church, seating 500 with standing-room for 200 more. The services, reported to be well attended, were conducted by Methodist, Independent and Baptist ministers.[4]

The total number of worshippers, although well below the aspirations of clergy and ministers at the time, is still remarkable compared with today's situation. 24,430 sittings, even if most were rented, provided for over half the population; and if all seats were rarely filled, the average attendances amounted to more than one third of Hull's inhabitants in 1834. It is, however, the contrast between Nonconformist success and the Established Church's comparatively feeble showing which is most striking. By the 1830s, Hull was largely a Nonconformist town.

The age and occupation of the inhabitants reveal the background against which the Churches worked. Over half the people in Hull were under 20 years of age at the time of the 1831 census. Only 10,907 males were aged 20 or over, and the social and political climate of their formative years was quite different from that of Hull's ageing clergy with their fearful recollections of the French Revolution. The preponderance of females over males suggests a settled, stable community. This may have been partly the result of the men's absence at sea, but there was also overcrowding and deprivation among the poor with only 9,000 houses among 12,000 families.

Trade and manufactures, the occupation assigned to the majority, is a broad category. Only 128 individuals were employed in manufacture or in making machinery for manufacture, but 5,653 were engaged in retail trade or handicrafts, masters and workmen. Another 2,620 were labourers, mostly in the docks. Hull was a port and commercial centre before it was a manufacturing town, remote from large centres of population and markets for manufactured goods.

The commercial development of Hull attracted entrepreneurs. Its upper class at the end of the eighteenth century consisted of a hundred or so merchant families.[5] About one in ten of the male population in 1831 (1,263) were 'capitalists, bankers, professional men and other men of education.' Wealth and position encouraged a few Nonconformists to join the Established Church, like Joseph Pease the Unitarian banker. Those who remained in retail trade created a Nonconformist constituency four times larger than the Church of England. Only Primitive Methodists could make much inroad among Hull's 2,620 labouring families, but by mid-century seven Wesleyan Methodist chapels provided five times more sittings than the Primitive Methodists, and attracted five times as many attendances. They also had over eight times as many communicants and over ten times the number of Sunday School children. These figures reflect Wesleyan Methodism's appeal to respectable lower middle-class families in retail trade.

The shortage of work for women in Hull is confirmed by the large number of female domestic servants, almost 2,000, about 16 per cent of the female population over school age. Only 136 men were servants, 29 of them under 20 years of age.

1851 Religious Census

Within twenty years of 1831 Hull's population increased by over 35,000 to a total of 84,690, and the number of church buildings doubled. Manufacturing industry developed, the railway arrived in 1840, and Railway Dock and Victoria Dock were built. Whale fishing had virtually ceased but trawling began when owners and crews from Brixham and Ramsgate migrated to Hull in 1845. By 1851 the port was in the early stages of its climb to prominence as a major centre for trawlers. The town had grown further to the north and west. Drypool, where Victoria Dock was built, was increasingly developed, but in spite of an enlarged population, the typical occupational pattern changed little between 1831 and 1851 (Appendix III).

The largest single group was engaged in some way with the transport of goods by ship and barge. On the night of the census, 30 March 1851, 2,060 persons were on board vessels in harbours, creeks and rivers. Hull was not a major shipbuilding town and only 623 men and boys were employed in the trade. Females still outnumbered males by over 4,000 and domestic service remained the most usual occupation outside the home for 3,649 women and girls. There were 126 nurses, five midwives and 428 charwomen. 1,689 milliners and 343 seamstresses worked mostly from their own homes while there were 206 schoolmistresses of varying ability. The arrival of the cotton and flax mills in mid-century gave Hull's women their first taste of factory work.

The Church of England's response to the development of the town between 1831 and 1851 was to increase its number of churches from eight to seventeen. The Independents still had six (not always in the same premises as before), Baptists, Roman Catholics, Quakers and Unitarians had one each. The biggest expansion was among Methodists. Wesleyan chapels increased from seven to ten, Primitives from one to five and New Connexion from one to two. The Independent Methodists were still in Osborne Street but their adult attendances increased from 350 to 1,300. Wesleyan Reformers, the Wesleyan Methodist Association and a variety of small Nonconformist bodies sprang up in the intervening years.

Few Churches could keep up with a population increase of 70 per cent in twenty years and in only two cases was the percentage increase in attendances greater than the population growth.

Primitive Methodist	80%
Roman Catholic	73%
Church of England	34%
Wesleyan Methodist	32%
Independent	17%
Baptist	no change

Combined Methodism increased its adult attendances by 57 per cent and with twenty buildings had more places of worship than any other denomination. Total Nonconformist attendances increased by just over 50 per cent. Hull appeared a strongly Nonconformist town with 39 chapels, providing twice the number of sittings of 17 Church of England centres and one Roman Catholic.

All Nonconformists	23,720	sittings
Church of England	13,808	sittings
Roman Catholic	648	sittings

Against the population increase of 70 per cent, Church attendances as a whole went up barely 40 per cent.

	1834 (1831 pop. 49, 361)		**1851** (pop. 84, 690)	
Church of England	7,600	(15%)	13,795	(16.4%)
Nonconformist	14,630	(29%)	27,575	(32.9%)
Roman Catholic	560	(1.1%)	2,050	(2.3%)

In 1851 Nonconformists were still twice as numerous as the Established Church's congregations, and their lead was increasing. Roman Catholics doubled as a percentage of the population but remained a small minority. Nonconformity added 5,790 sittings, the Church of England 4,008, at least a greater proportional increase since 1834 in terms of its own size.

Sittings

	1834	**1851**	**Increase**
Church of England	9,800	13,808	41%
Nonconformist	17,930	23,720	32%
Roman Catholic	600	648	8%

The 1881 Religious Census

There has been no national religious census since 1851 but thirty years later many towns in England began to hold their own, often published in a local newspaper. The *Hull News*, a paper sympathetic to Nonconformity, conducted a census on 27 November 1881. The results showed that from a population increase of 154,240 (i.e. 80%), an increase of 57% in church going in fact represented a percentage decrease of inhabitants attending public worship.[6]

Church of England	from 16.4% to	8.6%
Nonconformist	from 39.9% to	30.8%
Roman Catholic	from 2.3% to	1.6%
Total	from 58.6% to	41.0%

A total of 41 per cent, however, compared quite favourably with other northern towns in the 1880s: Darlington 35.4%, Barrow-in-Furness 33.8%, Stockton-on-Tees 31.8%, and

Warrington 29.2%. Even Wesleyans and Primitive Methodists, in spite of their spectacular growth in Hull, decreased slightly as a percentage of the population between 1851 and 1881.

Wesleyans   from 9.5% to 8.1%
Primitive Methodists   from 6.5% to 6.2%

The percentage of Nonconformists was still high compared with the Church of England and the Roman Catholic Church, helped by 11,394 Salvation Army attendances on census day. The Wesleyan chapels were virtually full, a little over three-fifths of Church of England pews were occupied, and Catholics filled their relatively few places of worship three times over.

The increase in attendances helped to mask the fact that some Churches were in relative decline. The Methodist New Connexion and the United Methodist Free Church each decreased by 12 per cent, Baptists by 25 per cent and Independents by 32 per cent.[7]

As Hull became more densely packed with the gridiron pattern of Victorian working-class streets, the Church of England built more churches. To St John's, St James', St Mark's and St Stephen's, all built before 1851, were added St Luke's (1862), St Matthew's (1872), St Barnabas' (1874) and St Jude's (1874). St Thomas' Church , a temporary building in Campbell Street in 1873 was replaced by a permanent church in 1882. St Andrew's, the only new church to be built in Drypool (1878), became the parish church ; St Peter's continued as a chapel of ease. Victoria Dock was built near St Peter's in 1850, but a greatly increased population in 1865 did not lead to increased congregations. The vicar, the Revd John Ellam (1863-76), attributed the falling numbers to a large influx of artisans who, he claimed, brought with them 'the confirmed habits of heathenish indifference to religious duties'.[8] The nearby Wesleyans, however, continued to make gains. In Sculcoates, where Christ Church and St Paul's were situated, All Saints' was consecrated as the parish church in place of St Mary's, the first church in Hull since the Reformation with no rented pews.[9] The mission church of St Clement's was opened in St Paul's parish in 1879. St Silas' was opened in 1871, St Philip's in 1885, and St Augustine's in 1896. St Saviour's on Stoneferry Road, a consolidated chapelry for St Mark's district in Sutton parish, was consecrated in 1903.

Most of these churches disappeared long ago, victims of war damage or departed congregations. Among the 'fallen' were St John's, Christ Church, St James', St Stephen's, St Paul's, St Jude's, St Thomas', St Andrew's, St Peter's, All Saints', St Silas', St Mark's, St Saviour's and St Augustine's.

Even greater numbers of Nonconformist chapels suffered the same fate, partly because many more were built in the first place. Methodists were the most prolific of church builders. They erected buildings, hired, bought and sold others and used school rooms with such alacrity that nobody can be sure how many premises were in use at any given time. It is likely that 106 Methodist chapels, mission rooms and school rooms were used as centres of worship up to 1914.[11]

After St Charles' Church was opened in 1829, Catholics concentrated on building schools and used school chapels for worship. St Mary's Church in Wilson Street was built in 1891 to replace a school chapel dating from 1856, St Patrick's in Spring Street, built in 1906, replaced a school chapel in Mill Street, registered in 1871. St Wilfred's in Boulevard was opened in 1896, the last Catholic Church to be built before the First World War.[12]

However it was Nonconformity, especially Methodism, which made the greatest appeal to the people of Hull. Baptist numbers were never great and Congregationalism was overtaken by the rising tide of Victorian Methodism. Shopkeepers, artisans and businessmen who came to Hull to seek their fortunes were most likely to be Methodist, if they belonged to any Church.

The Onset of Serious Decline

In the winter of 1903-4 the *Hull News* launched yet another religious census. Nonconformist ministers, especially Primitive Methodists, were enthusiastic, but the Anglican clergy were reluctant to take part. It would do no good, they said, and only tell them what they already knew. Evangelicalism in the Church of England was in national decline by this time, partly as a result of losing the intelligentsia and some of the middle classes. Nonconformity, on the other hand, was still able to draw its strength from its sectarian self-sufficiency and the voluntary religious commitment of its members.[13] The census was never completed. Only twelve out of thirty Anglican places of worship were enumerated; one Catholic school chapel was overlooked; one Congregational chapel, four Wesleyan, one New Connexion, six Primitive Methodist, a number of other Nonconformist places of worship, and almost all the Salvation Army, were not enumerated. The size of the task, the lack of enthusiasm on the part of the Church of England, and possibly the winter weather, proved too much for a small band of voluntary enumerators.

Hull's population increased more than three-fold to 277,991 between 1851 and 1911 and its inhabitants continued in the same or similar occupations. Over 11,000 were in metals, engineering and shipbuilding, but the largest occupational group, 32,000, were in broadly commercial occupations, the conveyance of goods, people or messages by rail, road or water, including 8,000 dock workers. A smaller number were employed in making furniture and fittings, in timber, dressmaking, hotels and lodging houses, in law, medicine and teaching. There were 2,526 retired persons listed as 'not Army and Navy.' 1,070 enjoyed private means and the largest single group among those 'without specific occupations,' 83,491, included scholars and students from ten years upwards.[14]

The 1903-4 Religious Census, albeit incomplete, confirmed that Hull was still a decidedly Nonconformist city. Even if the Church of England's recorded attendances were doubled, they would have been only half the Nonconformist attendances, themselves also incomplete. All Churches combined accounted for 14 per cent of the population in the County Borough. If twice as many had attended, an over generous estimate, 28 per cent would have been distinctly worse than the position of 1881. Middlesbrough, a Victorian port and a centre of heavy industry on the Tees estuary, held its own religious census in 1904. It discovered that only 23 per cent of its people were church or chapelgoers. Both towns were predominantly Nonconformist although Middlesbrough had a much larger Roman Catholic minority, but Anglo-Catholic Middlesbrough and Evangelical Hull had similar causes for concern.

Holy Trinity was the only instance of the Church of England in Hull with over 1,000 attendances, but five Wesleyan chapels had over 1,000 each, including Kingston Chapel near St Peter's, Drypool where 119 attended. Congregations at St Stephen's and St Mary's, Sculcoates were only half those of 1851. They were less fashionable districts than sixty years before.

The three-fold increase in population was more than matched by an increase in clergy, ministers and other Church-workers, from 76 in 1851 to 301 in 1911, but their efforts to attract people to church could not keep pace with the rising population. On the contrary, the percentage attending public worship in Hull in the first decade of the twentieth century fell to half that of 1851. If children and afternoon services are omitted, and if allowance is made for congregations not enumerated in 1904, the decline of the Church of England and Nonconformity as a percentage of the population becomes clear.

	Church of England	Nonconformist	Overall
1834	13.8%	25.8%	39.6%
1851	13.0%	26.6%	38.6%
1881	8.9%	30.2%	39.1%
1904	6.7%	13.1%	19.8%

The Church of England held its own in the rising tide between 1834 and 1851, then began to fall away sharply. Nonconformists increased steadily up to 1881 only to drop alarmingly by 1904. Combined Church of England and Nonconformist attendances fell by over 20 per cent in twenty-three years. (Appendix IV shows Church of England, Nonconformist and Roman Catholic adult religious attendances in Hull for 1834, 1851, 1881 and 1904.)

What had gone wrong?

In the first half of the century Hull's Evangelicals were distracted from their declared priorities. They gave endless time and effort to anti-Catholic activities and attempts to resist Puseyism. In the second half of the century, as will be seen, there was a long and bitter fight with Nonconformists over education. These activities were by no means confined to Hull and are impossible to quantify. One cannot know what might have been the case if circumstances had been different.

The second half of the nineteenth century also saw the spread of agnosticism in England, which Charles Smyth attributes partly to the heavy demands Evangelicalism made on the clergy in the discharge of their parochial duties, leaving them little time to study and keep up to date with new social and intellectual trends.[15]. Evangelical otherworldliness did not encourage such habits, hence the revolution in the textual criticism of the Bible, in science and in historical studies was not adequately faced. The threat of Hell, once the most awesome weapon in the Evangelical preacher's armoury, was losing its effect. Calls for moral revival lost their force in the light of a doctrine of everlasting punishment which raised questions about the morality of the Bible itself.

Even the Establishment, so beloved of Evangelicals, proved a mixed blessing. It was difficult to maintain Evangelicalism and Established religion within a Church encumbered by State religion, and the difficulty became more apparent with the passage of time. Nonconformity, untroubled by this dichotomy, was Hull's dominant religion for the larger part of the nineteenth century. Anglican Evangelicals and Dissenters held similar theological positions but conflicting political opinions. Dissenters were more naturally radical in politics, and irked by the privileges of the Established Church. The Church of England regarded itself as the spiritual support of the traditional order and the bulwark of the nation against social chaos. Dissenters and Roman Catholics seemed to Evangelicals to be intent on importing alien and undesirable influences into England's social and religious culture. The middle-class nature of Congregationalism and the conservatism of Wesleyan Methodism did little to assuage Anglican fears.

There was, however, a conflict between devotion to the religious Establishment and the demands of serious religion. Joseph Milner had preached a Church which was a closed society, demanding total and exclusive allegiance to its doctrines and values. The world to him was at best a distraction from serious religion, a temptation and a snare for the easy-going and unwary. Evangelical Nonconformity preached an equally all-embracing doctrine of the Church, but unhampered by any real or imagined responsibility for State religion, it drew its strength from its own sectarian self-sufficiency.[16] Nonconformity was a subculture with no interest in integrating the dominant culture with the practice of religion. The personal religious satisfactions it offered made possible a withdrawal from the world without the dualistic tensions experienced by the Established Church . It was, therefore, a double irony that the very freedom which Nonconformity eventually won for itself became a main factor in its downfall. The removal of disabilities and a rise in the social and economic status of its members made Nonconformity a less attractive haven for the underprivileged. By the turn of the century Nonconformity in Hull was at the peak of its prestige. From such pre-eminence its subsequent collapse has appeared even more catastrophic than that of the Church of England.

VII

Keeping the Sabbath

Serious religion aspired to regulate the way everybody behaved on Sunday, whether they went to church or not. There was a time when all forms of Sunday work, sports and pastimes were matters of contention, but the 1677 Sunday Observance Act, much invoked in Hull in the nineteenth century, only prohibited labour and retail trade. Exceptions were made for works of charity and the sale of milk and meat to inns and cookshops; the insidious nature of the Act lay in the way it encouraged people to inform on one another, a widespread practice among most Evangelical societies up to the First World War; in Hull until almost the Second World War.[1] A Declaration for the Better Observance of the Sabbath was made at the accession of William and Mary in 1689, and the increasing influence of Evangelical opinion resulted in another Sunday Observance Act in 1780 which raised the five-shilling fine of 1677 to £200 on all who charged admission to organized Sunday amusements.[2]

Joseph Milner's fears concerning the irreligious effects of commercialism lived on in the Revd John Scott, Dikes's first curate and later vicar of St Mary's, Lowgate (1816-34). For Scott the worst consequence of commerce was the 'profanation' of the sabbath by both rich and poor. He urged the labouring classes and men of business to see the sabbath as a merciful institution, without which the labourer's life was 'one unvaried scene of abject drudgery.' Sunday was at least a relief after six days of such unenviable activity. If men of business worked on Sunday they became 'debased in mind, and wholly swallowed up in low-thoughted cares.' Even to think about business on Sunday, said Scott, was a violation of 'the sacred rest'[3], but for all his uneasiness about commercial life Scott, like most men of his time, felt obliged to accept things as he found them, wealth for some and drudgery for the majority. He only wished they would desist from drudgery on the sabbath. The ideal Evangelical Sunday was a form of weekly retreat, one day given over completely to quietness and prayer.

Leading citizens of wealth and position were expected to set an example to the lower orders. Sunday travel in Scott's opinion, 'proclaimed one's disregard to every rustic in every village through which one's conveyance passed.' He hoped that if the better-off entertained their friends on Sunday, as they frequently did, it was not mere entertainment. They should not prevent their servants from attending church and he hoped their own discussions were about what they had heard in church that morning, before returning again in the afternoon. Even going for a walk on Sunday could be dangerous, unless it were a retired and contemplative walk. Scott feared it would more likely be a mingling with crowds of 'the gay, the thoughtless, and the giddy'[4]. The majority in Hull had no choice but to spend their meagre spare time in the crowded streets. Scott's impracticable demands required a large house in the suburbs with a private garden attached. Even the fields on the outskirts of the town, where crowds of youths gathered for petty gambling, afforded no escape from worldly things.

Scott, like many Churchmen before and since, attributed all deficiencies in virtue to the decline of religion and family life, and he never shrank from proffering advice to those who were responsible for the lower orders.[5] Sunday evening was the time when servants, apprentices and other young people were allowed out for visiting and amusement, most of them according to Scott, spending the evening in the streets. He feared that more young women were ruined on the streets of Hull then than at any other time, where they met seafaring youths boarded out with people who exercised no control over them.[6] If only the higher classes would set an example to the lower orders in keeping the sabbath, he lamented, but not many among them were seen in church on a Sunday afternoon. As soon as the morning service was over they went into the country and wasted the day in 'self-indulgence, unprofitable conversation and amusement'.[7] This state of affairs prompted Scott to appeal to the magistrates and 'the respectable part of the community' to support the establishment of a society for the suppression of vice, on the lines of one recently formed in London.

Scott's Evangelical perfectionism had little hope of realization. The rich were absorbed by the thriving businesses which increased their riches while the poor, living in over-crowded tenements with no privacy, worked until late on Saturday and rose late on Sunday. For the majority of domestic servants Sunday evening was their only free time and they were unlikely to find their way into the pew-renting churches with their fashionable, predominantly female congregations at Holy Trinity, St Mary's and St John's.

Twenty years later the poor, who still had only the streets and the public houses for recreation, appeared to have no interest in organized religion or religious education; many did not bother to send their children to Sunday School.[8] For the better-off there were the increasingly popular Sunday steam-packet trips, the times of sailing announced by the town crier on a Saturday evening. These recreations, in contrast with those of the poor, were unlikely to be legislated against and the fresh air of the estuary must have been a relief, to those who could afford it, from the pervasive stench of the slums. Conditions in Hull's new areas were even worse than in Old Town, which at least had the advantage of standing raised on several centuries of its own waste. In most new working-class areas every ditch became an open sewer after heavy rain.[9] The magistrates, however, concentrated on bringing the lower orders into line, like one George Munroe, sentenced to three months on the treadmill for teaching boys the art of juggling on a Sunday.[10]

The issue of Sunday travel was a simple matter when few owned their own 'conveyance,' but new and more widely available means of travel introduced some contradictions into the sabbatarian cause. There were two Sunday trains in each direction on the Hull to Selby Railway, opened in 1840, four on weekdays. If there were no trains on Sunday then more coach and cab drivers were obliged to work. Many people who went to church on Sunday used their own carriages including, a letter writer reported in the *Hull Advertiser*, 'a leading zealot who had just preached on the subject, who then drove back to Newland in a private carriage, thus obliging his groom to work'.[11]

The zealots were undeterred by such anomalies, and no sooner was the Hull and Holderness Railway opened in 1854 than the clergy called a meeting to persuade the directors not to run trains to Withernsea on Sundays. E.F. Collins derided them in an *Advertiser* editorial, pointing out that anyone who employed a groom, coachman or cook on a Sunday was as much a sabbath breaker as a stoker or guard on a railway train. If people were out of Hull on Sundays, Collins concluded, they were at least away from the temptations of the dram shops and beer shops.[12]

The introduction of horse-drawn trams produced fresh enthusiasm for the sabbatarian cause, but the Hull Churches in deploring the running of a Sunday tram service in 1877 were soon hoist with their own petard. The Mayor, Alderman Edward Bannister, a wealthy coal exporter, informed the objectors that at least 1,000 people had urged him to put on Sunday trams to get them to church or chapel from the outlying areas.[13]

The clergy were in an ambivalent position. The Revd R.K. Preston, curate of St Mary's, in a sermon on the value of the sabbath, seemed unable to decide where he stood. He made so many exemptions and qualifications to allow for changing social conditions that he ended by sounding in favour of Sunday trams himself.[14] St Mary's under John Scott III was moving towards the Catholic revival in the Church of England and so was less concerned to maintain the purity of its one-time Evangelical doctrine. Even the Evangelical vicar of Holy Trinity, Canon Joseph McCormick, put humanitarian considerations before religious advantage at a Jubilee Breakfast in 1887 for tramdrivers, conductors and their families, remarking that as the men worked a 14-16 hour day, seven days a week, they ought to have a rest on Sunday, even if that meant fewer in the congregation at Holy Trinity.[15] When the Tram Company was taken over by the Corporation in 1899, the Sunday morning tram service was discontinued for a time in deference to clergy and ministers who objected. When the full-day service was restored, 20,000 fares were collected on the first four Sundays and the most crowded times were immediately before and after the morning hours of worship.[16] Sunday trams had advantages for Churches and for the Hull Corporation.

The Churches had their greatest sabbatarian successes over the issue of Sunday trading; the Corporation benefited again, this time because the more the Sunday Observance law was broken the larger the income from fines. The same people appeared before the bench time after time because a five-shillings fine under the 1677 Act was no hardship to the better-off tradesmen. Some regular offenders even offered to pay a year in advance to save the inconvenience of constant appearances in court. By 1882 two-thirds of all prosecutions for sabbath breaking in the United Kingdom (1,151) occurred in Hull.[17]

As usual the law bore down more heavily on the poor than the rich, and the Hull Radical Club enquired why small traders, tailors and sellers of fish were prosecuted rather than shipowners and tram companies.[18] Prosecutions at the end of the century were running at around 3,700 a year,[19] and Hull Corporation held the record for prosecutions of Sunday traders. Culprits ceased bothering to turn up in court to answer charges; a five shillings fine was acceptable as a small tax on profits,[20] and Hull Corporation was happy to draw an annual income of over £1,000 from these mutually satisfactory transactions.[21]

Fines were not increased, in spite of the Nonconformist *Hull News'* call for Sunday trading to be made more expensive. The Bench instructed the Chief Constable to apply costs, usually 4s.6d,[22] but this extra imposition could cause hardship for small traders. Benno Pearlman, the solicitor, took up the case of a widow who could not afford to close on Sundays and whose profits would be eliminated by the extra 4s. 6d..[23]

Large shops with much bigger profits than the widow in the back street were generally in favour of Sunday closing, and many who opened would have been glad to close if others had done the same. Frederick Needler, the Methodist confectioner and Sunday School teacher, said that the opening of shops discounted the work of Sunday Schools and he believed the evil would be reduced if costs were added.[24] It was common knowledge, commented the editor of *Hull News*, that most of Hull's traders supplied the youth of the city with sweets and tobacco.[25] The Revd A.B.G. Lillingstone, vicar of Holy Trinity, also thought the opening of shops on Sunday was bad for the young, adding tortuously that it 'caused children and young people to congregate on a day when they had perfect leisure, and created an element of excitement which was offensive and resulted in unnecessary and unwise expenditure of small sums of money.' He was also in favour of charging costs,[26] but the Bench gave discretion to the magistrates in order to avoid cases of undue hardship.[27] The Corporation, nevertheless, continued to draw an income from this source until a year or two before the Second World War.

There were almost 5,000 shops in Hull in 1911 and its reputation for a rigorous Sunday closure policy was greatly admired and widely quoted in other towns. The *Annual General Report of Hull District Chamber of Trade* in 1913 displayed a league table in which Hull was the clear winner in enforcing the 1677 Sunday Observance Act.[28]

	Population	Sunday opening
Hull	278,000	100
Liverpool	746,000	4,000
Manchester	714,000	4,000
Glasgow	784,000	3,344
Bristol	357,000	3,000
Bradford	288,000	1,200
Oldham	147,000	800
Blackburn	133,000	705
Burnley	101,000	550

If 5,000 shops served the regular needs of Hull on weekdays, only 100 open on a Sunday must have made shopping virtually impossible on that day. In the other towns it would have been merely inconvenient. But only the poor, as we have seen, needed to shop on Sundays and the proprietors of small shops in poor areas, who were unlikely to belong to the Chamber of Trade, were obliged to remain open seven days a week in order to make a living themselves.

A band playing in a public park on a Sunday afternoon was one of the quintessential sounds of late Victorian England, but not one which Hull Nonconformists liked to hear. They saw their Sunday Schools as training places for future god-fearing, upright citizens, and objected to band concerts during Sunday School hours. Five hundred signatures were sent to the Mayor and Council in 1888 from teachers and officers of the local Sunday School Unions, petitioning against this practice.[29] Another petition quickly followed from three Primitive Methodist Circuits with a total of almost 5,000 children in Sunday Schools.[30] The biggest petition came from the United Sunday School Committee, signed by 1,671 teachers and officials in Church of England and Nonconformist Sunday Schools, covering 79 sheets of note paper. In presenting the petition, the Revd John Hetherington, vicar of St Peter's, Drypool, declared his support for fresh air and recreation and recognized that modern society was emancipating itself from long hours of toil. He hoped that 'the toiling multitudes' might have recreation and music to their hearts content, so long as it did not encroach upon 'those precious hours of Sunday School training'.[31]

The offending concerts usually stopped for a while after a petition, but once the fuss died down they started again. This in turn led to further petitions, spelling out more clearly the fears which such seemingly harmless events raised in the minds of Sunday School officials. Controlling the working classes had always been seen by the Established Church as one of its prime civic duties. Nonconformists in Hull, now drawn from the higher ranks of local society, saw it as part of their duty too. It was not simply that music in the parks on a Sunday led to the desecration of the sabbath; it was also 'subversive of the moral and spiritual welfare of the people'.[32] Nor was it just a matter of the bands tempting children to play truant. The Nonconformist Church Council feared that the large increase in Sunday traffic would imperil the quiet and orderly observance of the sabbath which was 'essential to the moral and physical well-being of the people'.[33] Workers when not at work tended to congregate in large groups with nothing to occupy their time. This spelled trouble to the respectable classes, the more so since Hull's recalcitrant populace was even less biddable to its religious mentors than formerly.

The Primitive Methodists made one more effort in June 1894, when bands were reintroduced in the parks after a break of a few weeks. A petition, signed by 1,464 persons over sixteen years of age, pleaded that young people would be tempted to neglect religious education, and this would lead to an 'utter disregard of the sanctity of the Lord's Day' and subvert 'the moral and spiritual welfare of the community'.[34]

The convulsions of the First World War greatly diminished local enthusiasm for the sabbatarian cause. Some, however, soldiered on under the leadership of Canon Berry, vicar of St Andrew's, Drypool (1914-47). It was largely through his efforts that prosecutions for Sunday opening continued. Up to the time of the 1937 Sunday Trading Act there were 26,000 prosecutions in England and Wales every year. All but 1,000 were from Hull or Grimsby.[35] Hull's reputation for unyielding sabbatarianism inspired the couplet,

> Of you who complain that Mentone is dull,
> Come to England and try a wet Sunday in Hull.[36]

VIII

Temperance

Sobriety was less important than keeping the sabbath among Evangelicals.[1] Drunkenness was denounced as a sin, but total abstinence was not demanded by the rich Evangelicals of Wilberforce's generation who kept good wine cellars and well-stocked larders. When Wilberforce took Stanstead Park for a few days his host, the Revd Lewis Way, remembered to leave him a case of port and an order for half a buck.[2] Many leading brewers were Evangelicals and their names appeared regularly on Church Missionary Society subscription lists in the 1830s: Guinness, Whitbread, Buxton, Hanbury, Hoare, and Perkins.[3] Later in the century Evangelicals were still chiefly motivated by religious objectives, by the urge to make converts rather than support for abstinence for its own sake.

Temperance, however, was one example in Victorian England where rival religious denominations were eventually able to work together in harmony. By the end of the century it had become 'the common ethical ground of all sects from General Booth to Cardinal Manning'[4], but an inherent inability to work with secular temperance bodies did the Churches much harm.

The crusade against alcohol began outside the Churches and continued on uneasy terms with them until after 1850. Religious people in Hull were suspicious of a movement, often associated with Friendly Societies, which displayed so many quasi-religious characteristics. The pledge sounded like a vow, and Evangelicals found co-operation difficult because the secularity of the movement seemed to suggest that moral reform was possible before or even without religious conversion.[5] Temperance developed an almost exclusively Christian flavour, but its casual connection with organized religion helped to hasten the secularization of religion. It was a 'religious' issue which could be pursued as effectively outside the Churches as it could within. Temperance also developed those aspects of Evangelical religious elitism, the dividing of the righteous from the unrighteous, which made them both unattractive to large numbers of the poor.

In spite of religious leaders' suspicions, a cross section of Dissenting ministers was closely associated with the temperance cause in Hull from the start. A small gathering in the Friends' Meeting House in Lowgate in 1831 included the Revd Charles Daniels of George Street Baptist Chapel, the Revd Ebenezer Morley, Independent, the Revd George Lee, the Unitarian editor of the *Hull Rockingham*, and the Revd Edmund Grindrod, Methodist. They were joined by Dr William Bodley and James Henwood, a banker's clerk who took the chair.[5] The new movement soon adopted the traditional style of a Nonconformist revival meeting where visiting speakers gave their testimony, chaired by a respected local citizen.

The British and Foreign Temperance Society was founded in the same year and employed missionaries to stump the country addressing public meetings. One such, the Revd J. Jackson, held a meeting in Fish Street Chapel at which a Hull spirit merchant announced that he was closing his business at the end of the month. Another result of Mr Jackson's visit was the formation of a Seamen's Temperance Society. The seamen sat in glum silence at the inaugural meeting, seeing it as yet another attempt by employers to control their lives. The Seamen's Friendly Society representative declared the scheme to be nothing more than a move by shipowners to deprive seamen of their comforts while sparing their own pockets.[6]

Teetotalism, total abstinence from alcohol, was established in Hull in 1835 by Richard Firth, proprietor of the Classical and Mathematical Academy.[7] A group of Nonconformist ministers, supported by a few respectable citizens like Firth, were the acknowledged leaders of Hull's early teetotal movement. There was still room for working class people but their chief value at public meetings, it had to be admitted, was to give testimony as reformed drunkards. It was not to be expected that prominent merchants would announce in public that they had been in the habit of drinking too much at the club. Drunkenness was more conspicuous in public houses or on the streets and the testimony of a reformed drunkard was one way of persuading others to sign the pledge, like four characters at the first meeting of Hull Sailors' Teetotal Society, established by the missionary to seamen, the Revd John Spencer.[8]

There was scope too for women. Four women from Leeds gave addresses and sermons at the first anniversary of the Female Temperance Society, but the occasion was still chaired by a man, the Hull raff merchant John Wade. The women were not allowed to preach on Church premises, only in the Court House or the Freemason's Lodge. The female branch, however, boasted 300 members who could enter 'places of misery and woe to which the male sex could not be admitted'.[9] Opportunities for female and working-class leadership were typical of Nonconformity, but a world away from the Church of England. Temperance reform revealed a difference between Anglicanism and Nonconformity as notable as that between Disraeli's two nations.[10]

The first mention of involvement on the part of the Established Church was when the non-doctrinaire Bromby, vicar of Holy Trinity, chaired a temperance meeting in the Court House for a fashionable following in November 1840. The galleries were reported crowded with women and several more 'of the middle class' occupied the bench.[11]

It was, ironically, a non-religious body, the Sculcoates Temperance Society, which first made an impact on the clergy of the Established Church when four of them took the pledge, without their names being divulged. The Sculcoates Society approached both rich and poor, respectable and disreputable, but kept them separate from each other. On Christmas Day 1848 a public meeting of 500 'respectable' members and friends took tea in the Mechanics' Institute with a local worthy in the chair, Henry Levitt, seedcrusher and oil merchant. In an adjoining room was another meeting addressed entirely by reformed drunkards, but there was no mention of tea.[12]

As societies multiplied, a Hull Temperance League was formed to co-ordinate activities and to control the rougher element. Open air meetings led to disorder and fighting with those who opposed temperance, so the League decided against holding such events in future. At first this seemed a backward step; the average indoor meeting without refreshments attracted no more than 100 people. This disadvantage, however, was soon overcome when Hull was visited regularly by nationally famous speakers. A visit from a well-known temperance speaker encouraged local enthusiasts, provided a memorable evening's entertainment, and produced a few more pledges in the hot-house evangelistic fervour of the occasion. After the speaker departed the local movement returned to its round of dull self-congratulatory meetings, drank tea, produced literature and remained generally out of touch with the homes of the poor.

J.B. Gough, Hull's most famous visitor, a reformed American drunkard who toured Britain on behalf of the National Temperance League, appeared in the town in 1854, 1855 and 1878. Gough's second evening at the Theatre Royal in

1854 was an especially dramatic occasion. So eloquent was his oratory that no sooner had he sat down than the Revd William Kemp, Dikes's curate and successor at St John's, was on his feet to announce his intention of taking the pledge, challenging the chairman, Alderman Blundell, the paint manufacturer, to do the same. Kemp was the first Evangelical clergyman to come out in the open and the Revd James Sibree of Salem Independent Chapel also declared his intention to sign the pledge. They were congratulated by Collins in the *Advertiser* for setting an example.[13] Statistics announced at Gough's meeting revealed that out of 2,119 people taken into custody in Hull that year, 486 (356 men and 130 women) were arrested for drunkenness; 117 of the men were poor labourers. The audience was further informed that 522 males and 233 females among those arrested could neither read nor write, 986 others only imperfectly. It was confirmation of the widely accepted connection between ignorance and crime, but if only ten per cent of the drunk and disorderly were actually arrested, as generally believed, there were 5,000 cases of drunkenness each year among Hull's 85,000 population at mid-century.

The respectable and religious, never niggardly in giving advice to the unrighteous, were less notable for their generosity in providing support for sinners. The Hull barrister James Burke could only raise £6 from a collection in the Town Hall to support the work of an Irish priest, Father Theobald Mathew (1796-1856), 'The Apostle of Temperance.' Only 100 subscribing members attended the annual meeting of the Hull Temperance League in 1855.[14]

The Revd William Kemp's example had no noticeable effect on his fellow clergy. The fact that others had started the temperance movement tended to make it something with which Hull's Evangelicals could not afford to be associated. Dissent and Catholicism were still synonymous in their minds with radical politics and subversion, and the notion of self-improvement without religious conversion was not something they wanted to encourage, so the Church of England kept to its own world for the time being. Distressing events sometimes occurred even inside that carefully guarded world, like the death from drink of the Revd John Farrand in 1863. Farrand lived in Tynemouth Street, was 46 years old and married. He had been turned out of his living for habitual drunkenness and had recently lived at Flamborough.[15]

The large-scale growth of temperance activity in Hull coincided with the growth of Nonconformist influence under the lay-leadership of men like Thomas Ferens and Joseph Rank, and reached its peak in the years leading up to the First World War. By then the Church of England in Hull was also fully involved and temperance had become almost exclusively associated with religious sentiment and organization. Many Evangelicals became teetotallers, but the movement itself never adopted the attire of Evangelicalism. Temperance sat lightly to all forms of organized religion and many secular bodies had their own temperance societies: railway workers, Friendly Societies and the like, but to be teetotal, if not a religious position, was at least to make a moral stand bordering on the religious.

The Band of Hope came into its own in the second half of the century and was taken up enthusiastically by the Churches. Formed in Leeds in 1847 as a society for juvenile abstainers, it quickly spread to all parts of the country and was adapted to the needs of Sunday Schools and other work among the young. It concurred with a traditional reaction of organized religion when faced with intractable moral problems; the only course was to make a fresh start with the rising generation. From the first Band of Hope Sunday in Hull in 1875, when six sermons were preached in the Church of England and other denominations, it became the most widely supported temperance activity associated with the Churches. The *Band of Hope Advocate*, a monthly magazine, was launched as the organ of the Hull and District Band of Hope League.[16]

Outside the Churches the main organizers of working-class temperance were the Friendly Societies. In Hull the *Temperance Pioneer* was reborn in 1892, after a gap of 55 years, as the quarterly magazine of the Hull Grand Division of the Sons of Temperance. The Churches looked on Friendly Societies as potential competitors. They were working-class movements which decided for themselves how far they wanted to associate with organized religion. The adoption of a neo-religious language, like the Sons of Temperance with their ranks of Grand Masters, Grand Sires, Worthy Patriarchs and Brothers, combined the features of a religious society with those of a trade union, more often associated by the Churches with political subversion than with pastoral care. The Sons of Temperance marched behind their banner at the annual Church parade and a branch, if it felt disposed, might invite a local minister to be its chaplain.[17] Local friendly societies struggled to survive through lack of business experience and felt the Churches had closed their doors against them. They usually held their meetings in public houses and so organized religion lost another opportunity of influencing the industrial masses.

The Liberal Government's Licensing Bill of 1906, an attempt to speed up the operation of Balfour's 1904 Act in reducing drunkenness through the limitation of licensed premises, was rejected at its second reading, but encouraged joint temperance work in Hull. A Hull Citizen's Committee was formed to support the Bill's proposals under its secretary Bertram Fox, district superintendent of the United Kingdom Alliance. The chairman was Robert Owen, a barrister, and the Revd Robert Harrison, superintendent of one of Hull's seven Primitive Methodist circuits, was treasurer. They were joined by a large number of representative citizens including 50 ministers and clergy, but only five were Anglicans. Hull had long been a Nonconformist city and the leaders of public opinion were a triumvirate of Methodist laymen, Thomas Ferens the Wesleyan industrialist, philanthropist and Liberal

M.P., Joseph Rank, the wealthy New Connexion corn miller with a house in London, and Alfred Gelder the architect and Hull's first town planner. Ferens and Rank had long been recognized leaders in Hull's temperance movement, and it was said that these three men designed, built and paid for most of the chapels of the period.

The Revd A.B.G. Lillingstone, vicar of Holy Trinity and a recent convert to the cause, also played a leading part in the campaign, but he needed an assurance that his participation would not identify him with party politics. The United Kingdom Alliance was too political, which meant too Liberal, for Lillingstone's taste. Established Churchmen in Hull were still nervous of risking religious or political contamination. Two mass meetings in support of the Licensing Bill were addressed by distinguished visitors from many parts of the country and 18,000 names and addresses were collected. The largest single subscription, £50, was from Ferens.

The petition was the climax of the 'big meeting' in Hull. Doubts were beginning to be expressed about its effectiveness, and when Bertram Fox wrote to Rank again in 1911 to seek his support for a conference of temperance workers, Rank expressed his doubts as to the value of such events. They only resulted in a lot of 'patting on the back.' Rank was in favour of a return to the methods of earlier days. Time would be better spent, he wrote, in direct temperance work, visiting people in their homes and persuading them to sign the pledge. He enclosed a donation of one guinea.[18]

It may be argued that habitual drunkenness was more damaging to persons, families and the community than opening shops or travelling on Sunday. Yet it is clear that sabbatarianism was a bigger issue in Hull because of the number of people it affected. It is also true that Hull, religious and secular, was more successful in dealing with what it saw as infringements of the sabbath. The temperance movement, however, is significant as an example of how a divided religious community, which began by ignoring the issue or by trying to pursue it on denominational lines, was in the end driven to co-operate. But the problem of co-operation between the secular and the religious was never finally resolved. The century ended with the religious arm of the movement diluted by association with the secular arm, but in command of the field.

IX

Prostitution

'This great social evil,' a much-used Victorian epithet for prostitution, was prolonged by the vast gap between riches and poverty in nineteenth-century society. It was often a last-resort means of income for the poor. Some rich men, schooled in the rigours of the counting house, ascribed it to the laws of supply and demand, while others found in prostitution an uncovenanted safeguard against the misappropriation of their wives and property. The typical beneficiaries of these transactions were poor women and rich men, supplemented in Hull by paid-off seamen on shore leave, temporarily flush with money and starved of female company. Some among the poor also seemed able to find money from somewhere for solace with prostitutes.

The Poor

When the Revd Newman Hall came to Hull in 1849 to begin his pastorate at Albion Congregational Chapel, a cholera epidemic was raging in which several thousands died. For the rest of his life Hall never forgot the funeral processions which passed his windows all day long and far into the night, deaths increasing from 40 to 700 a week. Religious services were held every night in churches and in the streets at which the pestilence was attributed to the sins of sabbath-breaking, infidelity, popery and drunkenness. Newman Hall later realized that a more likely cause lay in Hull's numberless houses crowded together for as much rent as possible without regard for sanitation, each newly built street quickly becoming an open water course.[1] Poverty and ignorance were at the root of the plague.

Written evidence from an enquiry by the clergy into the condition of Hull's working classes in the winter of 1849-50 painted a vivid picture of widespread poverty just above pauper level.[2] Seven thousand people in one district lived in old tenements, sunk and damp with a step down upon entering. Widows took in lodgers at 1s 6d a week, many between 16 and 18 years of age who had quarrelled with their parents. Over fifty women had been deserted by their husbands and mobs of dirty children, attending no school, roamed the streets until they started work at nine years old, the earliest age permitted by the Factory Acts. Single women lodged two, four or six to a house.

Even in the more respectable streets near Christ Church there were densely crowded areas where the inhabitants were glad to obtain any kind of work for two or three days a week. In the St Stephen's area many were temporary lodgers, moving on after a day or two. There were over 5,000 paupers in Hull at the time, but this did not reveal the full extent of poverty. Many eked out a precarious existence, often unable to obtain work, at other times in work which barely provided subsistence. Employment for the majority in Hull was intermittent or seasonal, depending on the state of trade or imports from northern Europe where the Baltic froze each winter.

By the end of the century slum conditions in Hull, as elsewhere in Britain, were even worse. Clergy and scripture readers investigated the condition of the poor again in 1883 under the leadership of the Revd Malet Lambert, vicar of St John's, Newland, a leading campaigner for education and sanitary reform. The worst conditions were near the docks where houses, packed into tiny courts, were let in single rooms. Each court was approached by a dark passage often ankle deep in sewer water which opened out into a court running left and right, bounded by filthy privies. A second passage led to a further court. Some occupants were labourers on 10s or 12s a week; others were hawkers of vegetables, rabbits, fish or other perishable articles. The rest lived from hand to mouth, 'begged, stole, held a horse or carried a box.' Only the eradication of such squalor, Malet Lambert concluded, could lead to moral improvement.

> So long as these crowded dwellings exist the poorest classes must necessarily be forced into them often in close contact with the most repulsive forms of vice. . . . These influences must be so continuous and powerful as to render an improvement in their physical condition a necessary prelude to any general moral or religious improvement.[3]

Lambert failed to draw Rowntree's conclusion, based on a study of poverty in York, where it was clear that no working-class housewife could provide the basic family necessities from her husband's wages alone. She was left with three possibilities if she were not to prostitute herself. She could starve herself and her children so that her husband, the breadwinner, had enough to eat, she could take in a lodger or take in work. In desperate circumstances she might attempt all three at once.[4] Rowntree cites the example of a shirtmaker who had five hours to make a shirt. If she started at six o'clock in the morning she might have three completed by nine o'clock at night, for which she was paid 4s a week less the cost of cotton and candles, leaving 2s 6d for a week's work of fifteen hours a day.[5]

Milliners, needlewomen and other females in low-paid occupations were often, as a consequence, associated in the public mind with prostitution. It is easy to understand the attractions of prostitution for an unmarried girl with no prospects of permanent employment; life on the streets at least offered an escape from poverty and might even provide the odd luxury, a new dress or an item of jewellery. Not for nothing were the female poor warned against 'love of finery.'

The Rich

The poor were likely to marry young or to experience sexual relationships outside marriage in an overcrowded slum tenement. Businessmen generally married late, after they had accumulated the wealth needed to set up the kind of matrimonial household expected of a successful man. Sex was pushed under the surface in respectable families. Young women grew up with little or no knowledge of the 'facts of life' and almost all recorded opinions on such matters were expressed in terms of male perceptions. Most respectable women, it was alleged, were not troubled by any sexual feelings. The dutiful wife submitted to her husband merely to please him and for the sake of having children.[6] The 'fallen' woman was condemned because she had tasted forbidden fruit and might make a habit of it. If she belonged to the servant class, thrown out by her employer and perhaps shunned by her family, prostitution was her only means of survival.

Continence, however, was not expected by everyone of the virile, late-marrying man of business. Here lies the source of Victorian sexual hypocrisy; the better-off were able to purchase sex from the poorer classes and at the same time condemn them for their promiscuity.[7] Women of middle-class households, wives, daughters and sisters, were the property of the husband and father, living under his authority; the prostitute was a defence, protecting his property and upholding the sanctity of family life.

> Herself the supreme type of vice, she is ultimately the most efficient guarantee of virtue. But for her, the unchallenged purity of countless happy homes would be polluted. . . . On that one degraded and ignoble form are concentrated the passions that might have filled the world with shame. She remains, while creeds and civilizations rise and fall, the eternal priestess of humanity, blasted for the sins of the people.[8]

The writer, W.E.H. Lecky, deplored the existence of 'not less than forty thousand unhappy women' in England, sunk 'in the very lowest depths of vice and misery.' These women he believed, nevertheless, protected the purity of the family, made certain the paternity of the children a man supported, and guaranteed the rightful inheritance of his property.

Such a frank admission is evidence of double standards and may account for the reluctance of Hull's property-owning classes to support efforts to combat prostitution. They dared not admit that prostitution was anything other than a foul and degrading vice, but the fact that it was 'unspeakable' made it a convenient form of security in a society ruled by mercantile considerations.

The Prostitutes

A deputation from the national Institute for Improving and Enforcing the Laws for the Protection of Women, on a visit to Hull in 1850, estimated the number of houses of ill-repute to be 5,000 in London, 355 in Dublin, 219 in Edinburgh, 200 in

Glasgow and about 200 in Hull.[9] If this was true Hull was in the big league, but estimates were sometimes no more than informed guesses and varied greatly. In *Prostitution in London* (1861), Mayhew and Bracebridge estimated that there were 80,000 prostitutes in the capital. Lord Gage, in an address to the Society for the Suppression of Juvenile Prostitution, believed there were 1,000 brothels in London and 100,000 prostitutes.[10]

Hull police returns between 1878 and 1888 record an average of 221 houses where prostitutes were accommodated, the number of prostitutes known to the police averaging 519 a year during the same period. By the First World War the number of arrests in Hull had dropped below 30. The fall in numbers might be attributed to a general rise in prosperity, but statistics for arrests, as in the case of drunkenness, are unreliable guides to what was actually happening. The increased number of ships passing through the port in the late nineteenth century would be likely to increase the demand for prostitutes. At the same time, compared with businessmen and merchants, a rise in commercial prosperity rarely improved the lot of the unskilled urban poor.

Many of the sea-going victims of Hull's brothel keepers were men from other ports who signed off in Hull and soon found no more than the rail fare to London or Liverpool remaining in their pockets.[11] Nor were Hull prostitutes always local. The streets were reported to be thronged with foreign pedlars and musicians, attracted by the delusion that England was a land flowing with milk and honey, and parents in the German states were warned of the numbers of girls taken to England every year for prostitution.[12] A Hull sailor procured a 17 year old German girl to work in the brothel kept by him and his wife, telling her she would be a servant in his public house.[13] Two other German girls, prosecuted for assaulting their employer, brought to light a thriving trade. A witness in the case, Johann Landherst, regularly brought girls from Germany, many of them settling in Scale Lane and Bishop Lane hard by St Mary's Church.[14]

Prostitutes and brothels were not confined to the dock areas; they could be found in almost any part of Hull, even in very respectable districts like Linnaeus Street. One brothel keeper who kept five houses in one street specialized in procuring very young girls. Five 'apprentice' prostitutes under 14 were found in another house,[15] and the trade became more blatant by the end of the century. Prostitutes openly paraded the streets near Paragon railway station from 11 o'clock in the morning until midnight, increasing in numbers as the day advanced and ending in drunken brawls after midnight.[16] The *Hull Critic* claimed there were a number of high-class prostitutes who were immune from police investigation.[17]

The majority of prostitutes were to be found in areas most associated with poverty where their clients were likely to be from the labouring classes,[18] augmented by paid-off seamen, as well as the rich. It is impossible to be accurate as to the number of prostitutes, or to know how many were part-time or gave false occupations when asked by investigators, but a modern researcher has suggested a way of identifying prostitutes from the Hull census returns.[19]

Young women in Hull on the night of the 1881 census were living with parents or with kin, in service, boarding, lodging, or visiting. Prostitutes were more likely to be boarders or lodgers.[20]. Female boarders were found mostly in respectable working-class districts; female lodgers generally occupied the overcrowded slum areas associated with prostitution.[21] An examination of Cook's Buildings, a crumbling eighteenth-century street, suggests that most of the 70 adult women were either prostitutes or brothel keepers.[22] If this was true, an average of 245 prostitutes proceeded against each year in the whole of Hull between 1878 and 1888 represented only a fraction of the total.[23]

The Church

The Revd Thomas Dikes, inspired by the launching of the Society for the Suppression of Vice in London in 1802, preached a sermon in St John's Church calling for a similar society in Hull.[24] William Wilberforce, associated with the society in London from its beginning, recognized the connection between vice and economic conditions. Hull's clergy were less percipient, but even the great Emancipator himself placed his emphasis firmly on the side of a crusade to purify the morals of the age.[25] The suppression of prostitution, however, came only third on the list of the society's aims, linked with private theatricals, fairs, dram shops, gaming houses, illegal lotteries and fortune-tellers.[26]

Hull's own Society for the Suppression of Vice was eventually established in 1807 after a sermon preached by the Revd John Scott before the magistrates. Its purpose was to enforce the laws against immorality 'when friendly admonition' failed.[27] Special efforts were made to discover and prosecute brothel keepers, but it proved impossible to make any real reduction in the numbers of prostitutes. The society's initial success encouraged the hope that a combination of informer and sympathetic magistrate would do for prostitution what it did for Sunday closing. The fines were much more severe in this case; two convicted prostitutes were sentenced to three month's solitary confinement.

Hull's clergy were obliged for a time to limit their attack on sexual sins to the pulpit. Their sermons, aimed primarily at the edification of their flock, became a form of popular entertainment like the lecture of a travelling temperance evangelist, but with the added attraction of prurience. A case of great notoriety in 1810 concerned Mary Lockham, a young woman of 19 who was charged with the murder of her illegitimate child, and was to be tried for her life at York Assizes. Notice of the forthcoming sermon drew such a crowd to the Sunday evening lecture at Holy Trinity, many being unable to get in, that the Revd John Scott's 'most impressive and pathetic discourse' was repeated the following Tuesday in St John's Church.[28] Scott's sermon showed pity and sympathy for the young woman, seduced and betrayed by her lover,[29] and he and Dikes visited her many times in Hull gaol before she was taken to York for trial, where she was acquitted. The fact that Mary was not a slut convinced Dikes of the 'awful consequences of debauchery'; no other sin, he believed, produced so many evil consequences.[30]

Scott, also convinced of the connection between seduction and prostitution, preached a sermon the following year in which he proposed the setting up of a Hull Female Penitentiary'.[31] The fearsome title made it clear where the preacher and respectable society laid most of the blame. Hull's first Penitentiary opened in Wincolmlee in 1811 and became the main weapon in Evangelicalism's fight against prostitution for the remainder of the century. On Dikes's death in 1847, John Scott II took over the leadership. The Penitentiary, unnoticed by many, opened and closed several times owing to shortage of money, while the well-off middle classes, through embarrassment or indifference, disregarded the clergy's appeals for support. Every time the Penitentiary was re-opened it catered for a larger area. Hull became 'Hull and the East Riding,' then 'Hull, the East Riding and North Lincolnshire.'

Entrants were expected to stay for two years, but numbers were very small compared with the number of known prostitutes; 489 were admitted between 1837 and 1865,[32] an average of about 17 a year, 145 were placed in service, 99 were restored to their friends, 86 were dismissed and 60 absconded. The success rate was barely 50 per cent, in spite of careful screening, and the regime was too strict for most. Hard manual work was required to cover the cost of food and clothing and to instil habits of self-discipline. The penitential exercises and the atmosphere of guilt and gloom were too much for all but those with the greatest powers of endurance.

Hull Temporary Home for Fallen Women, with accommodation for 16, was opened in Nile Street in 1861. Founded by the Revd Andrew Jukes, a Church of England clergyman turned Baptist, it was the only institution of its kind to survive into the 1890s.[33] Its aims were more limited than those of the Penitentiary and its name suggested less the need to be broken of habitual vice; nevertheless, a 'fallen woman' in Victorian England was regarded as little better than a prostitute.

In its determination to suppress vice Evangelicalism did not give enough attention to its prevention. Mrs L.K. Phillips, wife of the Evangelical vicar of St Philip's in Charlotte Street, discovered this at first hand when she disguised herself as a working woman and explored the conditions of the poor and friendless. After a day's work in a jam factory she and another employee searched in vain for a '4d doss' for the night, but there were no clean and respectable lodging houses in Hull for 'women only.' The Working Girls' Club was for those under 23, and the rescue homes were for those 'who wished to change their undesirable mode of life'. There were a number of places for men, the Church Army home and the Dockers' Lodging House, but a so-called furnished apartment was likely to be a bed, separated from several others by a sheet slung over a piece of string hung across the room. Only the lowest of the low made their homes in such lodgings and Mrs Phillips found the filthy conditions appalling. It meant that a respectable but homeless woman was obliged to go to a 'mixed doss.' Cheap and respectable lodging-houses were urgently required for 'women only' in Hull, and Mrs Phillips recommended that a capable woman should be appointed to inspect the licensed lodging-houses.[34] If Hull's Evangelicals had campaigned for this kind of accommodation, many more women might have been saved from prostitution.

The Churches in Hull had more success in enforcing Sunday observance than sobriety among the populace. They were least successful in their attempts to suppress prostitution. Those who chose to trade on Sundays were content to pay a modest fine, and the Corporation was glad to pocket it. The drink trade had vested interests which the Churches were powerless to resist, and any private excesses on the part of the well-off were less noticeable than those of the poor. More subtle and subversive forces were at work in the trade in human flesh, not least in the wretched poverty of the many and the ambivalent indifference of the rich. All types of Evangelical attempted to tackle the symptoms. The causes appeared to be beyond their influence.

X

Educating the Poor

The provision of elementary education in day schools uncovered some of the most far-reaching tensions between religion and social order in nineteenth-century England. An expanding population, the growth of industrial towns and the spread of new ideas, produced intense bewilderment which, paradoxically, found expression in bitter exchanges between opposing certainties. The rising urban working class undermined an hitherto unquestioned acceptance of rural England's social structures, where the Established Church was the dominant expression of religion and a partner in the maintenance of the status quo. These factors, combined with the impact of French political radicalism on English society, made the 1790s an historic turning point.[1]

Evangelicals saw themselves as the spiritual support of the old order. Dissenters and Primitive Methodists, on the other hand, were sympathetic towards radical politics as a means of breaking the Established Church's monopoly of religious, political and educational privileges. Wesleyans, Hull Wesleyans especially, long regarded themselves and were regarded by others as closely associated with the Established Church, but as the nineteenth century progressed disputes over education resolved their ambivalent allegiance. In the second half of the century the battle lines over education were drawn between the Church of England on one side and all Nonconformity on the other.

As England changed from an agricultural into an industrial economy, the new thinking which accompanied it comforted some Churchmen, but not others. The Evangelical J.B. Sumner (1780-1862), Bishop of Chester and later Archbishop of Canterbury, was greatly consoled by the economic doctrines of Adam Smith and Thomas Malthus, seeing them as synonymous with the will of God.[2] At the other extreme, the Tractarian Henry Phillpotts (1778-1869), Bishop of Exeter, had no faith in the lessons of political economy and grew increasingly fearful of the growing industrial lower class. The future looked grim, he said, for a nation of 'irreligious savages,' and he predicted a convulsive breakdown of social order.[3]

So the Church attempted to educate an illiterate population in the interests of religion and a stable society. The widely accepted cure-all character of education in the minds of the respectable was common ground for religious people, in spite of political or doctrinal differences. Education, it was felt, was the answer to widespread irreligion among the lower orders, and a remedy for the crime and disaffection of the young, removed as they were by urban streets and alleys from the traditional restraints of village life. The education of the poor, begun as a private charity in the eighteenth century and assisted by government grants from the 1830s, did not become a public service until 1870. By then the enmity between Established and Dissenting Churches, hardened into outright hostility, made co-operation in educating the poor and 'dangerous' classes impossible.

The expanding middle classes contributed to a number of educational initiatives in eighteenth and early nineteenth-century Hull. The Revd William Mason, vicar of Holy Trinity, founded the Vicar's School in 1730, assisted by a group of local tradesmen. It was rebuilt and enlarged by the Revd Thomas Clarke, Wilberforce's brother-in-law, in 1792 to take sixty boys for three years, nominated by himself. Alderman William Cogan founded and endowed a Charity School in Salthouse Lane in 1753 for twenty poor girls, the daughters of respectable people 'who would not sell ale or spiritous liquors or receive weekly allowances or ask alms, or let their children beg.' The school later provided marriage dowries for former pupils.[4] Trinity House Marine School, established in 1786, taught thirty-six boys writing, arithmetic and navigation. All boys apprenticed to a master mariner received free tuition.[5] 'Practical religion' was taught in a specially constructed loft in Holy Trinity Church.

Education affected only a minority in the mid-1780s, a few hundreds in a population of over 20,000, but as the population increased and trade expanded at the turn of the century, more wealth was contributed to education. A small group of professional people were among the earliest pioneers; they included John Alderson, the town's leading physician, the solicitors Charles Frost and John Broadly, the latter a member of a long-established banking and merchant family, Charles Lutwidge, the collector of customs, and George Lee, Unitarian minister and later editor of the *Hull Rockingham*. Four Sunday schools for boys and three spinning schools for girls were opened in 1786,[6] and a subscription charity school for boys and girls was opened in Carr Street, Sculcoates, in 1798.[7]

Mrs Lutwidge, wife of Charles Lutwidge and grandmother of Lewis Carroll (the Revd Charles Lutwidge Dodgson) became a leading figure in the new movement and, on her initiative, the Hull spinning schools were replaced by day schools for boys and girls in 1806 where larger numbers could be taught by the use of monitors.[8] Mrs Lutwidge also founded a Servants' School for older girls who were boarded, clothed and taught housework and reading. In 1818 the Trustees and Subscribers of the Sculcoates School decided to adopt the National System.[9]

As England's industrial towns continued to grow, more teachers were required than could be afforded. Two men, independently of each other, solved the problem by the use of 'pupil-teachers,' whereby older scholars instructed the younger ones. Dr Andrew Bell, an army chaplain in India, came up with the idea in 1789; a few years later Joseph Lancaster, a Quaker, started a school in London based on the same method. Each claimed to be the inventor of the system and considerable rivalry grew up between them. The quarrel soon became involved with religion. Bell, an Anglican clergyman, was for Church teaching and the Church Catechism; Lancaster believed in the non-sectarian teaching of 'general Christian principles and them alone'.[10] Bell's followers formed the Church of England National Schools; the Nonconformist British Schools were the outcome of Lancaster's ideas, but the instruction of younger children by older scholars became a common practice in both types of elementary school.

The motivation for educating the poor combined social, political and religious aspirations. The Church of England saw education as a civilizing process, ensuring the stability of society and an acceptance of the Establishment. It was an antidote to religious and social radicalism and aimed to direct those children into the Church whose parents were beyond its reach. Merchants and manufacturers also had a vested interest in the education of the poor for the sake of social stability, but it should not go too far and give the poor ideas above their station. Then they grew discontented with a life of drudgery. Since children in Hull left school between the ages of nine and ten, they had reason to be discontented.[11]

Below the more or less respectable poor was a growing underclass which neither National nor British Schools could reach. The Ragged School movement, associated with the name of the seventh Earl of Shaftesbury, was created to cater for this class, spurred on by the widely published statistics linking poverty and ignorance with crime.[12] Hull's Ragged School, opened in 1849, made little impact on the problem and was not popular with the Corporation, always parsimonious over educational matters. When it became possible to send boys to Reformatory School without previous imprisonment, Hull's city fathers feared an increase in pauperism if they saddled themselves with the maintenance of a school which only encouraged parents to neglect their children. The better-off lived in mortal fear of helping the undeserving poor, but Hull's leading citizens underestimated the longevity of destitution and its effects. The Ragged School built in Marlborough Terrace, later known as the Truant School for boys, did not close until 1909. A similar school for girls in fashionable Park Avenue closed as late as 1920.[13]

Apart from charitable and Church-provided education, by mid-century there was a large private, free-enterprise sector which benefited the middle classes, like Benjamin Snowden's long-lived Mercantile Academy and the Classical and Mathematical Academy founded by Richard Firth. A quarter of the child population, however, was still being educated in dame schools, the same number as in Church of England schools. Not only were many of the former receiving no education at all, but for too high a proportion of those who were it was of little or no value. Dame schools were no more than child-minding establishments for working parents and the 'dames' were unfitted for their alleged duties.[14]

Members of all classes in Hull in the 1850s were convinced of the need to educate the poor and some, including the poor themselves, began to look towards the government rather than the Church. A meeting in support of William Fox's Bill to promote secular, non-sectarian education received a petition from 500 Hull working men.[15] The Mayor, Thomas Palmer, was in the chair, supported by two Dissenting ministers and other prominent citizens. No Church of England clergy were present. The feeling of the meeting was that the Churches, at odds with each other, had only themselves to blame for education slipping out of religious control. The clergy offered a 'Church' education, based on the Catechism, emphasising the need for loyalty to the current religious and political establishments. Dissenters offered a broad religious and moral education based on the principles of religious freedom, leaving 'sectarian' matters to parental choice. Wesleyans were nearer to the Dissenting position, but in any case Church and Dissent combined could not have coped with the increasing numbers of children. What education the children did receive, observed the Mayor's meeting, was extremely poor and only equipped them for the most menial tasks. Many children missed out altogether and others spent an inadequate amount of time at school, even by the standards of the day.[16]

The idea of non-sectarian education did not appeal at all to Hull's Evangelical clergy, and they were incapable of understanding why Church of England schools seemed sectarian to Nonconformists. In any case, the Nonconformist and Established Churches combined could have provided a complete education for only a small proportion of the nation. Even Catholic schools could not cope with their own numbers after the Irish immigration. The Churches, however, were still the only providers of education but their disagreements, hardened by the passage of time, made it impossible for them to work together. There was even division over educational matters within the Church of England itself associated with the controversies between Evangelicals and Tractarians. Matters came to a head in 1853 when between 200 and 300 Evangelical clergymen walked out of the National Society's annual meeting and formed a society of their own.[17] The newly formed society held a meeting in Hull, as yet untouched by Tractarianism, in January 1854.[18] Protestant-Catholic rivalry inside the Church of England, which was to weaken and distract it for a century to come, was thus ushered into Hull in connection with education, a matter of common concern to all Churches as well as to a much larger number for whom theological disputation meant nothing.

The 1870 Elementary Education Act

It was obvious by the 1860s that the voluntary efforts of clergy, ministers and philanthropists, even when augmented by government grants, could not keep pace with the educational needs of the poor. The Newcastle report of 1861 revealed the shortcomings of popular education in every part of England and prepared the way for W.E. Forster's Bill of 1870. The government chose a compromise between those who urged it to abandon the denominational principle in favour of 'unsectarian' education and supporters of the religious principle. Forster's Bill aimed to provide a sufficient number of schools which were open to government inspection, but allowed complete religious liberty. Denominational schools were left alone where they were working well and meeting local needs. If this were not the case then locally elected school boards were given the power to levy rates, build schools and provide teachers. The Bill, which became an Act in August 1870, was limited to children under thirteen, but it did not provide free education; only parents who could not afford to pay were excused fees.

Canon Richard England Brooke, vicar of Holy Trinity (1868-75) was the chief protagonist on the Church of England side in Hull. He believed the denominational system had made the greatest contribution to the education of the poor, and feared that Forster's Bill was an attempt to divorce religion from education.[19] The Revd W.W. Statham, a Congregational minister newly arrived in Hull, took the lead in supporting unsectarian, free, compulsory education.[20] The replacement of voluntary denominational schools by rate-aided secular schools promised to rid Nonconformity of the disadvantages it had long suffered, arising from the privileged position of the Church of England, but there was a strange lack of enthusiasm among Hull's Nonconformists to join in the battle for religious liberty. Brooke put forward a proposal accepting Forster's Bill and adding a conscience clause to allow denominational instruction on parental request. Statham, as his fellow Nonconformists were reluctant to act on their own, was obliged to agree.[21]

Not all Evangelicals shared Brooke's enthusiasm for denominational schools. The vicar of Christ Church, the Revd Field Flowers Goe, John King's curate and successor, was among them. A man of some distinction, Goe was appointed Rector of Sunderland then of St George's, Bloomsbury before becoming Bishop of Melbourne. He was anti-Catholic and a convinced Evangelical, but he never showed animosity towards those who held different opinions from his own. Hull Nonconformists were gratified when he declined nomination to the School Board in order to save an election.[22] Goe was convinced that secular education would come and he believed Sunday Schools were the way to 'inculcate religious truths into the minds of the juvenile poor.' Brooke's suggestion that religious instruction should be given to the children by their own minister would have introduced sectarian strife into the National Schools; there was already more than enough bickering among the Churches at this time.[23]

At a meeting with the Town Council, radicals and Nonconformists were far from satisfied with the Education Act. They feared it still embodied the interests of sectarianism and denominationalism, and that the Church of England would turn even rate-aided schools into 'centres of propaganda for its creed.' They had been deluded, they said, by the notion of unsectarian teaching, which simply meant every sect teaching its own creed. The privilege of reading the Bible in schools had been preserved at the price of 'catechism and creed teaching'.[24]

There was endless manoeuvring for sectarian advantage over the selection of representatives to serve on the new School Board. In the end the Church of England was the strongest single group, but Nonconformists had eight places among them. There was a Roman Catholic, one 'working man,' J.T. Upton, a tailor, and a book-keeper from the Reform Union. It was a victory for Nonconformity and anti-sectarianism. At the first meeting of the Board Sir Henry Cooper, the physician, was elected chairman, a post which Brooke coveted. Sir Henry, although Church of England, was acceptable to all. Brooke was not. He stood for election as vice-chairman, but this time was beaten by nine votes to four by Thomas Stratten, a Nonconformist fruit merchant.[25]

The 1902 Education Act

If a Liberal Education Act failed to solve Nonconformist problems, little could be expected of a Conservative government. School Boards had at least provided a way of working together and accommodating differences, but Balfour's Act of 1902 exposed the irreconcilable depths of religious divisions in Hull.

The new Bill seemed to Nonconformists to reverse the main principles of the 1870 settlement by giving rate-aid to the teaching of 'denominational dogma' in elementary schools. They feared, rightly as it transpired, that the Bill would revive the bitterness of 1870 all over again, and if state-paid teachers were to be made subject to sectarian tests, the majority of appointments would be closed to Nonconformist teachers, and parents in rural areas would find it even more difficult to obtain education for their children without exposing them to religious opinions contrary to their own.[26] Much of the opposition in Hull was led by members of the Quaker Reckitt family and Thomas Ferens, the Wesleyan director of Reckitt and Sons, later Liberal M.P. for East Hull and principal founder of Hull University College.

Nonconformists had four grievances. The Bill struck at the principle that public expenditure should be accompanied by public control. It proposed to levy rates in support of schools where 'sectarian dogmas' were taught. It deprived men and women of their constitutional rights, which they had enjoyed for thirty years, of electing School Boards and serving on them. It imposed religious tests on citizens who were otherwise qualified to be teachers.[27]

Their objections were overridden, the Bill became an Act and protest turned into resistance. It began in rural areas, chiefly among Primitive Methodists, where Evangelicals joined the High Church Party in attacking the rights of Nonconformists. Methodists felt the Evangelicals had betrayed them.[28] A Hull and District Passive Resisters' League was formed by those who refused to pay the school rate and shortly afterwards large numbers of resisters gathered in Beverley where sixteen men and four women were to be summoned before the courts.[29]

A High Court ruling to accept part-payment did not prevent the distrainment and sale of household effects, often affording entertainment for the unfeeling bystanders at outdoor markets. Primitive Methodists in Hull, however, were prepared to go to gaol rather than pay what they regarded as an unjust rate. The Revd William Bowell, secretary of the Hull Passive Resisters' League, was imprisoned in Hull Gaol for five days, spending his time sweeping the prison paths, raking gravel or reading in his cell where he was visited by the governor and the chaplain. On the morning of his release ministers and friends gathered outside the gaol at a quarter past six. Bowell, as was the custom, had been sent out before breakfast. Mrs Bowell provided him with cocoa and sandwiches; there followed speeches and hymns, including 'Dare to be a Daniel', sung with great heartiness.[30]

The Revd Nathan Jefferson, superintendent at Clowes' Chapel, and the Revd J.A. Alderson of Ebenezer Chapel were sent to prison in 1905. Arrested during a missionary service in Clowes' Chapel, they were in Hull Gaol before the service was ended and two laymen, one elderly, were imprisoned with them for three of four days.[31] Such treatment was in accordance with the law of the land, but it helped to sour relations between Nonconformity and the Church of England for many years to follow.

The Apotheosis of Established Religion

The Liberal landslide of 1906 marked the peak of Nonconformist influence in England. Augustine Birrell, president of the Board of Education, was the son of a Baptist minister and well aware of the feelings of Free Churchmen, particularly over the Church of England's monopoly in village schools. The logical way out of the educational impasse was to start again from first principles. The choice was either total secularization or the teaching of everyone's religion on equal terms. The first was against the religious tradition of the nation, the second would have been an administrative nightmare. Birrell decided to build on existing foundations and a new Education Bill was brought before the House of Commons in April 1906. It proposed to abolish the dual system and replace it with a single system under local authority control.[31]

The news created uproar in the Church of England in Hull. A high-powered protest meeting was held in the Assembly Rooms, chaired by the ageing Suffragan Bishop of Hull, Richard Frederick Lefevre Blunt, one time Archdeacon of the East Riding (1875-97). He was supported by William Joynson-Hicks, a leading Evangelical and president of the National Church League, a politician and lawyer who defeated Winston Churchill in the North West Manchester by-election in 1908. Joynson-Hicks was the Home Secretary who was to play a prominent role in the defeat of the Prayer Book Measure in 1927. There were thirty-four others on the platform, including

High and Low Church clergy, the Revd Malet Lambert, the Revd Scott Ram from St Mary's, Lowgate, the Revd A.B.G. Lillingstone, H.J. Toor of the Lincolnshire House of Laymen, John Nicholson, head of Thomas Stratten School and other Hull laymen.

The Bishop was in favour of religious teaching in schools by teachers who believed in it, according to parental wishes. Thomas Hall-Sissons, the paint manufacturer, a self-proclaimed 'Hull man and a life-long Churchman,' wanted to abolish the dual system in favour of equality for all forms of religious teaching. The 1906 Bill in his opinion endowed only Nonconformity.

There were those who still feared Nonconformist political radicalism even at this late stage. Colonel Arthur Knocker Dibb of the Militia, Managing Director of Hull Brewery Company, was in favour of Christian unity and hoped for the time when all Protestants would work together, but there were two classes of Nonconformist. There was the man they all respected and could be associated with, the God-fearing Nonconformist. The other type, declared Dibb to loud applause, was the political Dissenter. The Colonel and other speakers denied, as a matter of course, that they themselves spoke in any party political sense and H.J. Toor rejected the charge that opposition to the Bill was either political or clerical.

The Revd A.B.G. Lillingstone produced figures to prove that Holy Trinity and Drypool parishioners wanted Church teaching in school for their children. 'Sunday School teaching was not enough on its own', said Colonel John Travis-Cook, another Militia officer, of the solicitors Thompson, Cook and Babbington. Travis-Cook supported his argument by referring to T.H. Ferens' admission that only ten per cent of Sunday School children became chapel members. The meeting, which began with the Apostles' Creed and the Lord's Prayer, ended with a verse of the National Anthem,[32] just like Mrs Gilbert's social gathering with Hull's Anglican Evangelicals in 1817. In

1906, however, Dissenters were not invited. One who tried to speak from the floor was immediately ruled out of order by the Bishop. 'This was a meeting of Churchmen', said Blunt.

The Government had a majority of two to one when the Bill received its third reading in December, but it was emasculated by Tory back-benchers in the House of Lords who wanted to ensure the Church of England's dominance in rural areas. As a consequence the Bill was withdrawn.

The education of the poor was arguably the most important issue facing the Churches in Hull in the nineteenth century. All set great store on its civilizing properties and its ability to reduce vagrancy and crime by preparing young men and women to do useful work in the world. Evangelicals, particularly, saw education as a prerequisite for 'serious religion and the improvement of public manners,' yet education proved to be deeply divisive. Political and social divisions, rather than doctrine, ensured that the Churches in Hull which claimed to be Protestant and Evangelical ended the century further apart than they were when it began. The 1902 Act was a victory for the Church of England; Passive Resistance was Dissent's last great battle.[33] The Church of England in Hull, though numerically weaker than Nonconformity, enjoyed the fruits of that victory, for 1902 signalled the emergence of a form of 'Church education,' in spite of the Board Schools, which was to last for another half century.

XI

A House Divided

The Churches in Hull were opposed by two counter-cultures. One was impervious to religion, antichristian and associated with crime and vice. The other counter-culture, often found among the poor, tried to order its life according to the Christianity imbibed at Sunday School and Day School, but chapel or church-going was rarely part of its Christianity, as the religious census figures show. The poor could not see the point of the antagonism between the denominations, and were largely indifferent towards organized religion.

There was great disparity between rich and poor in Hull. The rich, whose wealth came mostly from commerce, gave a public allegiance to religion and to the values it fostered, and so ensured their own privileged positions and the continued prosperity of their businesses. They expected the poor to know their place, to be respectful, sober and industrious. Education, it was widely believed, was the best way of improving the morals of the poor, so long as it did not go too far and give them ideas above their station. If the children of the poor were educated in accordance with their social status, they would grow into God-fearing citizens without the undesirable criminal tendencies of a section of their class, and to the great satisfaction of Churchmen and businessmen.

Such hopes were not without foundation, given the low standards in the most basic elements of education among those whose careers landed them in Hull gaol. Ignorance was equated with criminality in the popular mind. But Hull's poor were trapped in a nexus of disadvantage, and their poverty was made worse by the seasonal nature of employment in a port whose main trade was with the Baltic. Many of the poor lived in the slum conditions which so appalled the Revd Malet Lambert in 1883 and convinced him that an improvement in their physical condition was a necessary prelude to any moral or religious improvement. Many parents could not afford to send their children to school, unless it were to a Ragged School, while others removed their children from school at the earliest possible age in order to supplement the family income. As a result most children were so ill-educated that they were unsuited for any but the most menial tasks and trapped in a cycle of poverty. Ignorance meant poverty, which sought relief either from charity or from crime. Vice and drunkenness were also endemic in Hull, as they were in all major seaports; there was a great deal of prostitution in Hull for a town of its size, and it would continue so long as the great disparities between wealth and poverty remained.

Much of Hull proved an intractable environment for the cultivation of religion. The minimum degree of respectability which would have made the poor feel welcome and at home in church was beyond the reach of most, and the demands of sabbath observance expected by the clergy were all but impossible for the majority who worked long hours and were paid on a Saturday night. The gap between the Churches and the poor was greater at mid-century, when the Churches which had once laboured among them moved up the social scale and became respectable themselves. The counter-culture has tended to prevail in the long term, and the increasing ineffectiveness of organized religion in Hull was made worse by rivalry among the Churches over politics and the education of the poor.

Joseph Milner may have owed his Evangelical conversion to the Countess of Huntingdon's missioners in Fish Street Chapel, but the French Revolution cooled his warmth towards Dissenters whom he suspected of radicalism. His successor as leader of Hull's Evangelicals, Thomas Dikes, believed that Dissenting hostility towards the Establishment was a permanent stumbling block to co-operation between the Church of England and Dissent, even over matters where they were of the same mind, such as the distribution of Bibles among the poor. The Established Church, for Dikes, was the guardian of civil society; its religious services were calculated to maintain peace and happiness, truth and justice, religion and piety. And although Dikes was strongly anti-Catholic, he saw no purpose in an alliance with Dissent against Rome.

Hull's Dissenting businessmen, conservative in politics, resented the unfair privileges of the Establishment, which for long had denied them public office. The French Revolution made life for Dissenters more difficult because, whether they had supported the Revolution in its early stages or not, they were suspect to the Establishment; at best they risked Government disfavour, at worst mob violence.

The successful expansion of Dissent in the first decade of the nineteenth century increased the Establishment's suspicions and dislike. The clear lead of Dissenters over the Church of England in Hull as early as 1834 would have made the latter a junior partner, at least numerically, in any rapprochement between Church and Dissent. But the failure of these separate strands of Evangelicalism, so close to each other socially and politically, to act jointly in providing for the religious and social needs of the growing town was a handicap from which they never recovered. The Dissenting desire for freedom of religion was confused in the minds of Churchmen with imported ideas of democracy, which they feared would result in the collapse of the social order.

Eighteenth-century Methodism ministered chiefly to artisans and the poor, and remained part of the Church of England during Wesley's life time. It continued a similar ministry during the first half of the nineteenth century, and many Methodists in Hull continued to see themselves as very close to the Church of England. But Methodism, like Old Dissent, was politically suspect from the Establishment's point of view because it was closely associated with significant numbers of the politically conscious artisan class. Methodists also protested their political loyalty and denounced radicalism. At the same time, after the religious dynamism of Methodism burst out of the confines of the Established Church and fractured into separate pieces, combined Methodism became the largest religious body in Hull. There were almost 12,000 Wesleyans and 9,000 Primitive Methodists attending chapel each week by the end of the century, and Wesleyans were the Liberal Nonconformist Establishment of Hull in place of the once dominant Tory Evangelicalism.

Old Dissent began outside the Church, Methodism from within. Dissenters, although of similar social standing to Anglicans, remained outside. Methodists departed from the Established Church as a Society, and grew into separate Churches, but by the end of the nineteenth century Nonconformity generally had become respectable, and the poor were outside the influence of most organized religion.

In spite of its obsessive fears of Catholic aspirations, the Church of England in Hull was never able to form an alliance with Nonconformity against Rome. It seems that social and political differences prevented the possibility of an anti-Catholic alliance between the Church of England and Dissent in the period 1829-1850, even in the face of the supposed Catholic threats to supplant the Established Church and to place a Catholic monarch on England's throne. Nonconformists like the Revd Newman Hall of Albion Congregational Chapel, meanwhile, although anti-Catholic in outlook, were charitably disposed towards individual Catholics who, like themselves, seemed to be mainly seeking religious freedom.

Fear for the safety of the established order remained at the root of the Church's distrust of Dissenters until about 1850. In the second half of the century, education became the chief bone of contention and arguably the main reason which drove Church and Dissent into mutually hostile camps for another half century. The clergy believed it was their inalienable right, as ministers of the Church by Law Established, to educate the poor. Only so could they be kept in order, have a proper respect for those set over them, and be inculcated with the doctrines of true religion. When it became obvious that the demands of universal elementary education were too great for the resources of the Churches, even when supplemented by government grants, the Church of England and Nonconformity fought each other bitterly, each side attempting to gain the greatest advantage for itself. After the Education Acts of 1870 and 1902, the Church of England still saw itself as the rightful guardian of the nation's morals, beginning with its responsibility to educate the poor. The clergy believed that the so-called privileges of the Establishment were vested in the Church for that high purpose. Nonconformists, on the other hand, wanted religious freedom and the right to educate their children in their own way. The resulting bitterness spilled over into civil disobedience when certain Primitive Methodists chose to go to prison rather than pay the compulsory education rate.

Throughout the period considered in this study, there were men and women on all sides who were prepared to commit themselves unreservedly to what they believed to be right, but matters which divided them seemed more important than those which they held in common. In the end neither Church nor Chapel, the latter at the pinnacle of its power and influence, could foresee the approaching collapse of organized religion. Hull's Churches, divided, vulnerable and on the threshold of a century of decline, continued to be chiefly occupied with their own internal denominational affairs.

Appendix I

Church and Chapel Attendances 1834*

Denomination	Chs	Sits	Attend	Comm	S/S
Par. Chs.	4	4,300	2,400	248	1,200
C. of Ease	4	5,500	4,000	520	-
Total C of E	8	9,800	6,400	768	1,200
Independents	6	5,750	3,100	783	666
Baptists	3	1,700	1,000	320	199
Wes. Meth.	7	5,530	4,760	2,540	1,339
Prim. Meth.	1	1,250	1,000	300	126
Ind. Meth.	1	750	350	100	-
New Conn. Meth.	1	1,000	700	300	220
Quakers	1	300	150	-	-
Roman Cath.	1	600	450	350	90
Unitarians	1	500	300	60	120
Swedenborgians	1	500	250	?	-
Sailors' Chapel	1	600	350	-	-
Jews	1	100	40	-	-
Total Nonconf. and others	25	18,630	12,450	4,663	2,760

*   T. Stratten, *Review of the Hull Ecclesiastical Controversy*, p.44

Chs	-	Number of churches and chapels
Sits	-	Number of sittings
Attend	-	Average Sunday attendance
Comm	-	Number of regular communicants
S/S	-	Number of Sunday School children

Appendix II

Social structure in the eighteenth century – Joseph Massie's enumeration of 1760

A. Spiritual and temporal lords, baronets, knights, esquires, gentlemen.

B. Clergy, lawyers, those in liberal arts, civil, naval and military officers.

C. Freeholders, farmers.

D. Merchants, tradesmen, innkeepers.

E. Manufacturers.

F. Labourers, husbandmen, cottagers, seamen, fishermen, common soldiers.

All Methodism 1740-90

A	B	C	D	E	F
1.4	2.5	12.1	7.6	47.7	29.1

England 1760 (Massie)

| 1.2 | 4.4 | 24.8 | 12.6 | 20.9 | 36.6 |

The percentage of 'manufacturers' among Methodists was twice as numerous as in the country as a whole.

C.D. Field, 'The Social Structures of English Methodism: 18th-20th Centuries,' *The British Journal of Sociology*, 28 ii (1977), p.218.

Appendix III

Hull Occupation Lists – 1851 Census (pop. 84,690)

Clergyman	31
Protestant Minister	34
Priests and other Religious Teachers	11
Barrister	1
Solicitor	65
Other Lawyers	20
Physician	8
Surgeon	57
Other Medical Men	42
Parish Clerk	3
Other Church Officers	8
Law Clerk	86
Law Court Officers and Law Stationers	15
Druggist	181
Others dealing with drugs and surgical instruments	6
House proprietor	87
Merchant	161
Banker	8
Ship Agent	81
Broker	22
Agent or Factor	12
Salesman	3
Auctioneer	33
Accountant	32
Commercial Clerk	412
Commercial Traveller	82
Pawnbroker	32
Shopkeeper	43

Hawker or Pedlar	129
Other General Merchants, Dealers and Agents	141
Railway Driver, Stoker and others	216
Coach or Cab Owner and all engaged in Road Conveyance	259
Canal Service and Inland Navigation	1358
Ship Owner	61
Seaman	2268
Others connected with sea navigation	804
Warehousing, messengers, porters, etc.	701
Building and fitting ships/barges	623
Labourer (branch unidentified)	2150
Independent means	132

Appendix IV

Adult Religious Attendances

	Church of England	Nonconformist	Roman Catholic
1834	6,400	11,960	450
1851	11,906	24,380	1,650
1881	13,772	46,556	2,414
1904	6,438	23,859 ·	4,258
(incomplete)			

Population

1831	32,958
1851	84,690
1881	154,240
1901	240,259

Notes

Chapter I

1. Pastoral Letter from all Humberside Church Leaders, 13 October 1985.
2. Edward Royle, *Modern Britain: A Social History 1750-1985* (London, 1987), pp.291f.

Chapter II

1. J. Lawson, *A Town Grammar School* (published for The University of Hull by Oxford University Press, 1963), p.163.
2. L.E. Elliott-Binns, *The Early Evangelicals: a religious and social study* (London, 1953), p.313.
3. R. and S. Wilberforce, *The Life of William Wilberforce* (London, 1838), I, p.7.
4. I. Milner, 'An Account of the Life and Character of the Author,' prefixed to Joseph Milner, *Practical Sermons*, I (4th ed., London, 1814), p.lviii.
5. *Ibid.*, p.xxiii.
6. *Ibid.*, p.xxxiii.
7. John King, *Memoir of the Rev. Thomas Dykes* (sic), (London, 1849), pp.36-7; 257.
8. Reginald Coupland, *Wilberforce* (London, 1945), p.33.
9. William Richardson (ed.), *Milner's Sermons*, II (York, 1808), Preface.
10. *Milner's Sermons* I, p.25.
11. *Ibid.*, p.57.
12. *Ibid.*, pp.152-3.
13. *Ibid.*, p.223.
14. *Milner's Sermons* II, p.73.
15. *Ibid.*, p.264.
16. Luke 16, vv.19-31.
17. *Milner's Sermons*, II, p.271.
18. *Ibid.*, p.273
19. *Ibid.*, pp.315-17.
20. *Ibid.*, p.323.

21.   Boyd Hilton, *The Age of Atonement* (Oxford, 1988), pp.115-16.
22.   Wilberforce, *Life of William Wilberforce*, II, p.228.
23.   King, *Dykes*, pp.225-7.
24.   *Ibid.*, pp.245-7
25.   *Ibid.*, p.222.
26.   *Hull Advertiser*, 18 December 1829.
27.   King, *Dykes*, p.53.
28.   *Ibid.*, p.29.
29.   *Ibid.*, p.222.
30.   *Ibid.*, pp.45, 225.
31.   *Ibid.*, pp.111-13.
32.   *Ibid.*, p.135.
33.   *Ibid.*, p.172.
34.   *Ibid.*, p.226.
35.   *Ibid.*, p.398.
36.   *Ibid.*, p.147.

Chapter III

1.   R.W. Ram, 'The Political Activities of Dissenters in the East and West Ridings of Yorkshire 1815-1850' (unpub. MA Thesis, University of Hull, 1964) p.302
2.   *Ibid.*, p.79.
3.   C.E. Darwent, *The Story of Fish Street Church* (Hull, 1898), p.23.
4.   *Ibid.*, p.19.
5.   Ram, 'Political Activities', p.31.
6.   Darwent, *Fish Street Church* p.102.
7.   *Ibid.*, p.127.
8.   *Ibid.*, p.108.
9.   *Ibid.*, p.104.
10.   *Hull Rockingham*, 25 May 1811.
11.   *Proceedings of the Dissenters in Hull* (Hull, 1811), pp.10-11.
12.   *Ibid.*, pp.12-13.
13.   *Ibid.*, pp.14-17.
14.   Darwent, *Fish Street Church* p.111.
15.   Census, 1811.
16.   Darwent, *Fish Street Church* p.111.
17.   Ram, 'Political Activities', p.111.

18. Robert Hole, *Pulpits, Politics and Public Order in England 1760-1832* (Cambridge, 1989), p.123.
19. J.C.D. Clark, *English Society 1688-1832* (Cambridge, 1985), p.409.
20. Owen Chadwick, *The Victorian Church*, I (London, 1971), p.400.
21. Darwent, *Fish Street Church* pp.49-50.
22. Ram, 'Political Activities', p.7.
23. *Report of the Proceedings at the Public Meeting of Dissenters, 18 March, 1834* (Hull, 1834), p.6.
24. *Ibid.*, p.21.
25. *Ibid.*, pp.27-28.
26. *Ibid.*, p.32.
27. T. Stratten, *Review of the Hull Ecclesiastical Controversy* (Hull, 1834), pp.7-8.
28. *Ibid.*, p.12.

Chapter IV

1. F. Young and A.E. Trout, *Hull Times*, 31 October 1931.
2. W.H. Thompson, *Early Chapters in Hull Methodism 1746-1800* (London & Hull, 1898), p.17.
3. *Wesleyan Methodist Magazine* (1837), pp.885-9.
4. *Ibid.*, p.888.
5. Nehemiah Curnock, (ed.) *The Journal of the Rev. John Wesley, A.M.* (London, 1938), pp.20-2.
6. *WMM* (1837), p.889.
7. John Walsh, 'Methodism and the Mob in the 18th Century,' *Studies in Church History* (1972), p.218.
8. *Ibid.*, p.215.
9. *Wesley's Journal*, 6, p.30.
10. *Wesley's Journal*, 7, p.405
11. *Wesley's Journal*, 8, p.76n.
12. J.T. Wilkinson, 'The Rise of Other Methodist Traditions,' *A History of the Methodist Church in Great Britain*, II (London, 1978), p.278; J. Walsh, *HMGB*, I (London, 1965), p.279.
13. Thompson, *Early Chapters* p.65.
14. 'The Life of Thomas Taylor,' *Lives of Early Methodist Preachers*, 5, T. Jackson (ed.) (London, 1872), p.72.
15. *HMGB*, II, pp.281-2.

16. Bernard Semmel, *The Methodist Revolution* (London, 1974), p.117.
17. *HMGB*, II, p.288.
18. *Hull Advertiser*, 22 April 1827; 30 October 1829.
19. *LEMP*, V, p.64.
20. R. Treffrey, *Remarks on the revivals in religion with brief notices of the recent prosperity of the word of God in Hull* (London, 1827), p.7.
21. *Ibid.*, p.7.
22. W.R. Ward, 'The French Revolution and the English Churches,' *Extrait de Miscellanae Historiae Ecclesiasticae*, IV (Louvain, 1972), p.78.
23. *Hull Advertiser*, 10 August 1795; 3 May 1796.
24. W.R. Ward, 'The Religion of the People and the Problem of Social Control 1790-1830,' *Studies in Church History* (1972), p.250.
25. *WMM* (1837), p.894.
26. *WMM* (1836), p.166.
27 S. Marriott, *An Outline of Methodist History in Hull 1746-1906* (Hull, 1906), pp.2-3.
28. S. Whitby, *Hull Worthies* (Hull, 1900), p.2.
29. *HMGB*, II, p.305.
30. Whitby, *Hull Worthies*, p.3.
31. Julia Stewart Werner, *The Primitive Methodist Connexion: its background and early history* (Wisconsin,1984), pp. 105-6.
32. *Methodist Conference Handbook* (1938), p.108.
33. *HMGB*, II, pp.310-11.
34. *Handbook*, p.109.
35. *Hull Advertiser*, 9 July 1824.
36. *Primitive Methodist Magazine* (1853), p.193.
37. *Ibid.*, p.194.
38. David Hempton, *Methodism and Politics in British Society 1750-1850* (London, 1987), p.14.
39. *WMM* (1836), pp.489ff.
40. Hull City Records, DCT/14; *Kelly's Directory of Hull*, 1903.
41. HCR, DCE/269.
42. HCR, DCW/352.
43. HCR, DCW/509; DCR/1/8/19.38.
44. Allison, K.J. (ed.), *The Victoria History of the County of York East Riding*, I Oxford, 1969), p.324.

45. David Neave, *Lost Churches and Chapels of Hull* (London, 1991), pp.48, 54.

Chapter V

1. Owen Chadwick, *The Victorian Church*, I (London, 1966), p.8.
2. *Hull Advertiser*, 16 and 23 January 1829.
3. *Ibid.*, 13 February 1829.
4. *Ibid.*, 20 February 1829.
5. *WMM*, March 1812.
6. William Hunt, *Hull Newspapers* (Hull, 1880), p.13.
7. *Hull Advertiser*, 27 February 1829.
8. *Ibid.*, 6 March 1829.
9. *Ibid.*, 30 September 1830.
10. *Ibid.*, 22 March 1838.
11. *Ibid.*, 14 February 1857.
12. David Newsome, *The Parting of Friends* (London, 1966), pp.250, 279.
13. *Ibid.*, p.390.
14. *Hull Advertiser*, 1 July 1854.
15. *Ibid.*, 9 September 1854.
16. *Ibid.*, 16 September 1854.
17. *Ibid.*, 22 November 1850.
18. *Ibid.*, 13 December 1850.
19. Basil Hall, 'Alessandro Gavazzi: a barnabite friar and the risorgimento,' *Studies in Church History* (1975), p.307.
20. *Hull Advertiser*, 22 March 1856.
21. Hunt, *Hull Newspapers*, p.15.
22. *VCH*, pp. 428-9.
23. *Hull Advertiser*, 22 August 1857.
24. *Hull Packet*, 11 September 1857.
25. W.L. Arnstein, *Protestant versus Catholic in Mid-Victorian England* (Missouri,1982), pp.108ff.
26. *The Times*, 4 February 1869.
27. *Hull News*, 20 February 1869.
28. *Ibid.*, 13 February 1869.
29. *Hull Times*, 27 February 1869.
30. *Ibid.*, 13 February 1869.

31.   *Ibid.*, 20 February 1869.
32.   *Ibid.*, 27 February 1869.
33.   *Hull News*, 13 February 1869.
34.   *Ibid.*, 6 March 1869.
35.   Alan O'Day, *A Survey of the Irish in England in 1872* (London, 1990), pp.65-6.
36.   Brian Little, *Catholic Churches Since 1623* (London, 1966), pp.66-7; 159.

Chapter VI

1.   *VCH*, p.215.
2.   *Enumeration Abstract 1831* (London, 1833), vol.II.
3.   *White's Directory of Hull* (1831), p.lix.
4.   *Ibid.*, (1838), p.598; J.J. Sheahan, *History of the Town and Port of Kingston-upon-Hull* (2nd ed. Beverley, 1866) p.612.
5.   Gordon Jackson, *Hull in the 18th Century* (Oxford, 1972) p.277.
6.   *Hull News*, 10 December 1881.
7.   Anon., *Thirty Years' Work in Connection with Prospect Street Church Hull 1868-1898* (Hull, n.d.), pp.3-4.
8.   York Diocesan Registry, R.VI.A.49; *VCH*, p.298.
9.   *VCH*, p.304.
10.   *White's Directory of Hull* (1882), p.95.
11.   *VCH*, pp.322-7.
12.   *VCH*, pp.331-2.
13.   David Englander, 'The Word and the World: evangelicalism in the Victorian City,' *Religion in Victorian Britain*, II (Manchester, 1988), p.35.
14.   *Census of England and Wales 1911* (London, 1913), vol. 10, part II.
15.   C. Smyth, 'The Evangelical movement in perspective,' *Cambridge Historical Journal* (1943), vol.7, p.162.
16.   A.D. Gilbert, *Religion and Society in Industrial England; Church, Chapel and Social Change 1740-1914* (London, 1976), p.140.

Chapter VII

1.   John Wigley, *The Rise and Fall of the Victorian Sunday* (Manchester, 1980), pp.24ff.

2.   *Ibid.*, p.26.
3.   The Rev. John Scott, *The Importance of the Sabbath* (Hull, 1808), p.27.
4.   *Ibid.*, p.31.
5.   *Ibid.*, p.39.
6.   *Ibid.*, p.41.
7.   *Ibid.*, p.42.
8.   *Hull Advertiser*, 7 March 1828.
9.   Bernard Foster, *Living and Dying: A picture of Hull in the Nineteenth Century* (Hull, n.d.), p.1.
10.   *Hull Advertiser*, 4 February 1831.
11.   *Ibid.*, 11 May 1846.
12.   *Ibid*, 15 July 1854.
13.   *Eastern Counties Herald*, 10 May 1877.
14.   *Ibid.*, 30 August, 1877.
15.   *Hull Trams* (Hull, n.d.), p.9.
16.   V. Fotherby, 'Sunday Observance in Hull 1870-1914' (unpub. B.A. Hull University Dissertation, 1977), p.36.
17.   *Eastern Counties Herald*, 13 April 1882.
18.   *Ibid.*, 18 May 1882.
19.   *Ibid.*, 12 January 1901.
20.   *Hull News*, 14 March 1903.
21.   Fotherby, 'Sunday Observance', p.20.
22.   *Hull News*, 15 May 1909.
23.   *Ibid.*, 7 August 1909.
24.   *Ibid.*, 24 July 1909.
25.   *Ibid.*, 15 May 1909.
26.   *Ibid.*, 27 July 1909.
27.   *Ibid.*, 7 August 1909.
28.   Fotherby, 'Sunday Observance', p.29.
29.   Hull Records Office, TCC/2/97, 24 August 1888.
30.   HRO. TCC/2/98, 3 September 1888.
31.   HRO. TCC/2/101, 9 May 1890.
32.   HRO. TCC/2/113/114/120, 3 May 1894.
33.   HRO. TCC/2/115.
34.   HRO. TCC/2/116, 7 June 1894.
35.   Richard Evans, 'The Social and Economic Structure of Hull' (unpub. Hull University Thesis, degree unspecified, 1936), p.254.

36.   Philip Harrison, 'Comments Out of Context,' (unpub. ms., Hull, 1966), p.12. Miles Smeeton, *A Taste of the Hills* (1961).

Chapter VIII

1.   Harrison, *Drink and the Victorians* (London, 1971), p.93.
2.   Ford K. Brown, *Fathers of the Victorians* (Cambridge, 1971), p.405.
3.   Harrison, *Drink and the Victorians*, p.59.
4.   K.S. Inglis, *Churches and the Working Class in Victorian England* (London, 1961), p.330.
5.   *Hull Advertiser*, 4 March 1831.
6.   *Ibid.*, 29 March 1833.
7.   *White's Directory of Hull* (1835).
8.   *Hull Advertiser*, 2 December 1836.
9.   *Ibid.*, 1 June 1838.
10.   Harrison, *Drink and the Victorians*, p.29.
11.   *Hull Advertiser*, 13 November 1840.
12.   *Ibid.*, 29 December 1848.
13.   *Ibid.*, 31 March 1854.
14.   *Ibid.*, 27 January 1855.
15.   *Hull Times*, 19 September 1863.
16.   Hull Central Library, L.178.05.
17.   HCL, L.178.06.
18.   HCL, Letter.

Chapter IX

1.   Newman Hall, *An Autobiography* (London, 1898), p.78.
2.   *Hull Advertiser*, 21 December 1849; 11 January 1850.
3.   *Eastern Morning News*, 2 November 1883.
4.   Fraser Harrison, *The Dark Angel* (London, 1977), p.173.
5.   *Ibid.*, p.174.
6.   Steven Marcus, *The Other Victorians* (London, 1971), pp.31-2.
7.   Harrison, *The Dark Angel*, p.242.
8.   W. E. H. Lecky, *History of European Morals from Augustine to Charlemagne*, II (London, 12th edition, 1897), p.283.
9.   *Hull Advertiser*, 20 August 1850.

10. Harrison, *The Dark Angel*, p.217.
11. *Hull Advertiser*, 11 January 1850.
12. *Ibid.*, 20 August 1847.
13. *Ibid.*, 9 September 1854.
14. *Ibid.*, 26 August 1854.
15 *Hull Critic*, 25 June 1885; 2 February 1884.
16. *Ibid.*, 6 June 1885.
17. *Ibid.*, 13 June 1885.
18. Frances Finnegan, *Poverty and Prostitution* (Cambridge, 1979), p.34.
19. E.M. Goldberg, 'The Life and Labour of Women in Hull in the 1880s' (University of Hull unpub. B.A. Dissertation, 1986).
20. *Ibid.*, p.29.
21. *Ibid.*, p.34.
22. *Ibid.*, pp.34-6.
23. HRO, Hull Police Returns.
24. T. Dikes, *On the Abounding of open Profligacy and Immorality* (Hull, 1804).
25. R.A. Soloway, *Prelates and People: Ecclesiastical Social Thought in England 1783-1852* (London, 1969), p.50.
26. Brown *Fathers of the Victorians*, p.429.
27. *Hull Rockingham*, 19 May 1810.
28. *Hull Advertiser*, 17 and 24 March 1810.
29. HCL, L.252.03.
30. King, *Dykes*, p.69.
31. *Ibid.*, p.75.
32. Sheahan, *History of Hull*, p.611.
33. *Bulmer's Directory of East Yorkshire* (1892), p.825.
34. L.K. Phillips, *The Ragged Edge, being Glimpses of Real Life in Hull* (Hull, 1908), pp.40-1.

Chapter X

1. J. Lawson, *A Social History of Education in England* (Oxford, 1963), pp.228ff.
2. E.R. Norman, *Church and Society in England 1770-1970* (Oxford, 1976), p.43; Soloway, *Prelates and People*, p.97; David McNally, *Against the Market* (London, 1993), p. 92.

3.   Soloway, *Prelates and People*, p.258.
4.   *VCH*, p.349.
5.   Gordon Jackson, *Hull in the Eighteenth Century* (published for the University of Hull by Oxford University Press, 1972), p.284.
6.   J. Craggs, *Guide to Hull* (Hull, 1817), pp.50-1.
7.   'Rules and Orders . . . Sculcoates Subscriptions Charity School 1789' (Wilberforce House Museum).
8.   'Proposals . . . for Affording a Suitable Education to the Children of the Sober and Industrious Poor 1806' (*Ibid.*).
9.   'At a Meeting of Trustees and Subscribers . . . 1818' (*Ibid.*).
10.   J.R.H. Moorman, *A History of the Church in England* (London, 1953), p.325.
11.   *Hull Advertiser*, 16 August 1844.
12.   *Ibid.*, 3 August 1849.
13.   *VCH*, p.357.
14.   *Hull Advertiser*, 26 March 1847.
15.   H.J. Burgess, *Enterprise in Education* (London, 1958), p.188.
16.   *Hull Advertiser*, 19 April 1850.
17.   Burgess, *Enterprise in Education*, p.142.
18.   *Hull Advertiser*, 13 January 1854.
19.   *Hull Times*, 15 January 1870.
20.   *Ibid.*, 10 February 1870; Burgess, *Enterprise in Education*, pp.192f.
21.   *Hull Times*, 28 May 1870.
22.   J.M. Meadley, *Hull Anglican Reformers* (Hull, 1981), p.21.
23.   *Eastern Counties Herald*, 31 March 1870.
24.   *Ibid.*, 12 January 1871.
25.   *Ibid.*, 2 March 1871.
26.   *Hull News*, 26 April 1902.
27.   *Ibid.*, 3 May 1902.
28.   *Ibid.*, 31 October 1903.
29.   *Ibid.*, 19 December 1903.
30.   *Ibid.*, 19 November 1904.
31.   Marjorie Cruikshank, *Church and State in English Education 1870-present* (London, 1963), pp.90-3.
32.   *Hull Times*, 2 June 1906.
33.   Alan Wilkinson, *Dissent or Conform?* (London, 1986), p.20.

Bibliography

Newspapers and Periodicals

Hull Advertiser
Hull Critic
Hull News
Hull Packet
Hull Rockingham
Hull Times
Eastern Counties Herald
Eastern Morning News
The Times
Wesleyan Methodist Magazine
Primitive Methodist Magazine
Hull Temperance Pioneer & Eastern Counties Chronicle

Directories

Battle's *Hull Directory* 1791
Bulmer's *Directory of East Yorkshire* 1892
Melville's *Directory of Hull* 1853
Kelly's *Directory of Hull* 1903
White's *Directory of Hull* 1831, 1835, 1846, 1882

Broadsheets and Pamphlets

Rules and Orders of Sculcoates Subscription Charity School 1787.
Hull Sunday Schools - Rules 1800.
Proposals . . . a Suitable Education to the Children of the Sober and
Industrious Poor 1806.
A Meeting of Trustees and Subscribers . . . 1818.

Unpublished Typescripts

Attfield, D., 'Church of England Social Survey' (Hull, 1981).
Evans, R., 'The Social and Economic Structure of Hull' (Hull
University B.A.Thesis, degree unspecified, 1936).

Fotherby, F., 'Sunday Observance in Hull 1870-1914' (Hull University B.A. Dissertation, 1977).

Goldberg, E. M., ' The Life and Labour of Women in Hull in the 1880s' (Hull University B.A. Dissertation, 1986).

Harrison, P., 'Comments out of Context' (Hull, 1966)

Ram, R.W., 'Political Activities of Dissenters in East and West Ridings of Yorkshire 1815-1850' (MA Thesis, Hull University, 1964).

Articles

Field, C.D., 'The Social Structures of English Methodism: 18th-20th Centuries,' *The British Journal of Sociology* 28 ii (1977), pp.199-225.

Gilbert, A.D., 'Methodism, Dissent and political stability in early industrial England,' *Journal of Religious History* (1978-9), pp.381-99.

Hall, B., 'Allesandro Gavazzi: a barnabite friar and the risorgimento,' *Studies in Church History* (1975), pp.303-56.

Walsh, J., 'Methodism and the Mob in the 18th century,' *Studies in Church History* (1972), pp.213-27.

Ward, W.R. 'The French Revolution and the English Churches,' *Extrait de Miscellance Historiae Ecclesiasticae*, IV (Louvain, 1972), pp.55-84.

Ward, W.R., 'The Religion of the People and the Problem of social Control 1790-1830,' *Studies in Church History* (1972), pp.237-56.

Smyth, C., 'The Evangelical movement in perspective,' *Cambridge Historical Journal* (1943), pp.160-74.

Relating to Hull and district

Abraham,W.H., *The Studies of a Socialist Parson* (Hull,1892).

Allison, K.J. (ed.), *The Victoria History of the County of York East Riding,* I (Oxford,1969).

Anon., *Thirty Years' Work in Connection with Prospect Street Church Hull 1868-1898* (Hull, n.d.).

Anon., *Hull Infirmary, The Story of, 1782-1948* (Hull, 1948).

Anon., *Hull Trams* (Hull, n.d.).

Arnstein, W.L., *Protestant versus Catholic in Mid-Victorian England* (Missouri, 1982).

Aveling, H., *Post Reformation Catholicism in East Yorkshire 1558-1790* (E. Yorks Local History Soc., 1960).

Baker. F., *The Story of Methodism in Newland* (Hull, 1958).

Brewer"s Dictionary of Phrase and Fable (London, 1981).

Carroll, Mother Austin, *Leaves from the Annals of the Sisters of Mercy,* III (New York, 1883).

Census of England and Wales 1911 (London, 1913).

Craggs, J., *Guide to Hull* (Hull, 1817).

Curnock, N., (ed.) *The Journal of the Rev. John Wesley, A.M.* (London, 1938).

Darwent, C.E., *The Story of Fish Street Church* (Hull, 1899).

Dickens, A.G., *Lollards and Protestants in the Diocese of York* (Hull, 1959).

Early Methodist Preachers, Lives of T. Jackson (ed.) (London, 1872).

Elliott-Binns, L.E., *The Early Evangelicals: a religious and social study* (London, 1953).

Entwhistle, Memoir of the Rev. Joseph, by his son (London, 1854).

Enumeration Abstract 1831 (London, 1833).

Freeman, C., *Mary Simpson of Boynton Vicarage* (E. Yorks Local History Soc., 1972).

Foster,B., *Living and Dying: A picture of Hull in the Nineteenth Century* (Hull, n.d.).

Fox, B., *Facilities for Drinking and Drunkenness* (Hull, 1906).

Gillett, E. and MacMahon, K., *A History of Hull* (Oxford, 1980).

Greenwood's Pictures of Hull (Hull, 1835).

Hadley, G., *New and Complete History of Hull* (Hull, 1788).

Hall, N., *An Autobiography* (London, 1898).

Hunt, W., *Hull Newspapers* (Hull, 1880).

Jackson, G., *Hull in the 18th Century* (Oxford, 1972).

King, J., *Memoir of the Rev. Thomas Dykes* (London, 1849).

Lawson, J., *A Town Grammar School* (Oxford, 1963).

Lawson. J., *Primary Education in East Yorkshire* (E. Yorks. Local History Soc., 1959).

Markham, J., *Streets of Hull* (Beverley, 1987).

Marriott, S., *An Outline of Methodist History in Hull 1746-1906* (Hull, 1906).

Meadley, J., *Hull Anglican Social Reformers* (Hull, 1981).

Methodist Conference Handbook (1938).

Milner, I., *An Account of the Life and Character of Joseph Milner* (London, 1810).

Milner, I. (ed.), *Milner's Practical Sermons,* I (London, 1814).
Neave, D., *Lost Churches and Chapels of Hull* (London, 1991).
Page, W.G.B., *History of Fish Street Church* (Hull, 1898).
Phillips, L.K., *The Ragged Edge: Glimpses of Real Life in Hull* (Hull, 1908).
Pryme, George, Esq. M.A., Autobiographic Recollections of, ed. by his daughter (Cambridge, 1870).
Richardson, W., (ed), *Milner's Sermons,*II (York, 1808).
Scott, The Rev. J., *The Importance of the Sabbath* (Hull, 1808).
Sheahan, J.J., *History of the Town and Port of Kingston-upon-Hull* (2nd ed. Beverley, 1866).
Stratten, T., *Review of the Hull Ecclesiastical Controversy* (Hull, 1834).
Thompson, W.H., *Early Chapters in Hull Methodism 1746-1800* (Hull, 1895).
Tickell, J., *History of the Town and County of Kingston-upon-Hull* (Hull, 1796).
Tomlinson, W.W., *The North East Railway* (Newcastle, 1914).
Treffrey, R., *Remarks on revivals in religion with brief notices of the recent prosperity of the word of God in Hull* (London, 1827).
Wilkinson,T., *The Wandering Patentee* (York, 1795).
Whitby, S., *Hull Worthies* (Hull, 1900).

General

Bebbington, D.W., *Evangelicalism in Modern Britain 1730s to 1980s* (London, 1989).
Brown, Ford K., *Fathers of the Victorians* (Cambridge, 1961).
Burgess, H.J., *Enterprise in Education* (London, 1958).
Carpenter, S.C., *Church and People 1789-1889* London, 1959).
Chadwick, O., *The Victorian Church* (London, 1971 & 1980).
Clark, J.C.D., *English Society 1688-1832* (Cambridge, 1985).
Coupland, R., *Wilberforce* (London, 1945).
Cruikshank, M., *Church and State in English Education 1870 - present* (London, 1963).
Davies, R., Raymond, G., Rupp, G. (eds.) *A History of the Methodist Church in Great Britain* (London, 1965, 1978, 1983).
Edwards, M., *After Wesley* (London, 1948).

Finnegan, F, *Poverty and Prostitution* (Cambridge, 1979)

Gilbert, A.D., *Religion and Society in Industrial England: Church, Chapel and Social Change 1740-1914* (London, 1976).

Harrison,B., *Drink and the Victorians* (London, 1971).

Harrison. F., *The Dark Angel* (London, 1977).

Hempton, D., *Methodism and Politics in British Society 1750-1850* (London, 1987).

Henriques, U., *Religious Toleration in England 1787-1833* (London, 1961).

Hilton, B., *The Age of Atonement* (Oxford, 1988).

Hole, Robert, *Pulpits Politics and Public Order in England 1760-1832* (Cambridge, 1989).

Hylson-Smith, K., *Evangelicals in the Church of England 1734-1984* (Edinburgh, 1988).

Inglis, K.S., *Churches and the Working Class in Victorian England* (London, 1961).

Kennedy, E. and Mendus, S. (eds.) *Women in Western Political Philosophy* (Brighton, 1987).

Langford, P., *A Polite and Commercial People - England 1727-1783* (Oxford, 1989).

Lawson, J., *A Social History of Education in England* (Oxford, 1963).

Lecky, W.E.H., *History of European Morals from Augustus to Charlemagne* (12th ed., London, 1897).

Little, B., *Catholic Churches Since 1623* (London, 1966).

Marcus, S., *The Other Victorians* (London, 1971).

McLeod, H., *Religion and the Working Class in 19th Century Britain* (London, 1984).

McNally, D., *Against the Market* (London, 1993).

Medhurst, K. and Moyser, G., *Church and Politics in a Secular Age* (Oxford, 1988).

Moorman, J.R.H., *A History of the Church in England* (London, 1953).

Newsome, D., *The Parting of Friends* (London, 1966).

Norman, E.R., *Church and Society in England 1770-1970* (Oxford, 1976).

O'Day, A. (ed.) *A Survey of the Irish in England (1872)*, (London, 1990).

Parsons, G. (ed.) *Religion in Victorian Britain*, II (Manchester, 1988).

Perkin, H., *The Origins of Modern English Society 1780-1880* (London, 1969).

Pollock, J., *Wilberforce* (London, 1986).

Price Hughes, H., The Life of, by his daughter (London, 1904).

Rowell, G., *Hell and the Victorians* (Oxford, 1974).

Royle, E., *Modern Britain: A Social History 1750-1985* (London, 1987).

Semmel, B., *The Methodist Revolution* (London, 1974).

Soloway, R.A., *Prelates and People: Ecclesiastical Social Thought in England 1783-1852* (London, 1960).

Sweet, J., *Revelation* (London, 1979).

Thompson, E.P., *The Making of the English Working Class* (London, 1968).

Venn, H., *Life of Henry Venn* (London 1834).

Walvin, J., *Victorian Values* (London, 1987).

Werner, Julia Stewart, *The Primitive Methodist Connexion: Its Background and Early History* (Wisconsin, 1984).

Wigley, J., *The Rise and Fall of the Victorian Sunday* (Manchester, 1980).

Wilberforce, R. and S., *The Life of William Wilberforce* (London, 1838).

Wilkinson, A., *Dissent or Conform?* (London, 1986).

Index

Lockham, Mary, 89
Lowthrop, Sir Henry, 22
St Luke's Church, 57
Lutwidge, Charles, 95

Manning, Henry Edward Cardinal, 42
Mariners' Church, 51
St Mark's Church, 57
St Mary's Church, Lowgate, 51
St Mary's Church, Sculcoates, 51, 60
St Mary's Roman Catholic Church, 58
Mason Street Chapel, 35
Mason Street Wesleyan School, 52
Mason, Revd William, 95
Mathew, Fr Theobald, 77
St Matthew's Church, 57
McCormick, Canon Joseph, 68
Mercantile Academy, 36
Methodism,
      arrival in Hull, 26
      New Connexion, 31, 57
      Primitive, 33-5, 109
      Wesleyan, 109
Middlesbrough, 60
Milner, Revd Isaac, 6
Milner, Revd Joseph, 6-9, 64, 108
Morley, Revd Ebenezer, 74
Motler, Fr John, 47
Musgrove, Most Revd Thomas, 44

National Temperance League, 76
Needler, Frederick, 69
Newman, John Henry Cardinal, 42

Nicholson, John, 104

occupations, 59
O'Neil, Augustus, 40
Owen, Robert, 79

Palmer, Thomas, 97
passive resistance, 102, 110
St Patrick's Church, 58
St Paul's Church, 58
Pawson, Revd John, 30
Payne, Revd George, 20
Pearlman, Benno, 69
Pease, Joseph, 53
St Peter's Church, Drypool, 51, 58, 60
St Philip's Church, 58, 91
Phillips, Mrs L.K., 91
Phillpotts, Rt Revd Henry, 94
population
      (1831), 50
      (1851, 1881), 54, 56
poverty, 50, 66, 82-85
Preston, Revd R.K., 68
prostitutes, 86-88
prostitution, 82-92
Providence Chapel, 52
Puseyism (see Tractarianism)

Raikes Street Chapel, 52
Ram, Revd Scott, 104
Rank, Joseph, 78-80
religious census
      (1851), 54-56
      (1881), 56-58
      (1904), 59-61
Roman Catholics, 3, 38-49, 58